CROSSWORD

Puzzle Book for Adults

Volume 1

For more fun puzzle books visit our Amazon store!

For US Puzzlers: bit.ly/rosenbladt
For UK Puzzlers: bit.ly/rosenbladt-uk

Copyright © 2020 Rosenbladt

Puzzle 1

ACROSS
1. A bubble
5. Meaningless chatter
9. Consumption
14. Hip bones
15. Italian currency
16. Less feral
17. Sharp pain
18. Too highly strung
20. Abstract being
21. Undeserved
22. Elderly, weak-minded people
24. As a substitute
28. Brink
29. Double curve
31. Scottish river
32. Bulk
33. Scottish lord
34. Vessel or duct
35. Ice-cream holder
36. Makes contented cat sound
37. Seasoning
38. Japanese sash
39. Stripped
40. Tins
41. Monetary unit of Romania
42. Regretted
43. Secular
44. Military organizations
46. Helms
49. Sauna
52. 13th letter of the Hebrew alphabet
53. Cooking measure larger than dessertspoon
56. Basic monetary unit of Ghana
57. More gelid
58. Sea eagle
59. Military detachment
60. Trifling
61. Printer's mark, keep
62. Egyptian deity

DOWN
1. Two-legged creature
2. Grassy plain
3. Transuranic element
4. Sack
5. Fair-haired
6. Exists
7. Region
8. German, Mr
9. Spoke
10. Gemstones
11. Atomic mass unit
12. Information
13. Work unit
19. Derides
21. Incite
23. Hoe-shaped axe
25. Promotion in rank
26. Freshwater ducks
27. Gusto
29. Rowed
30. Encircle
32. Staid
33. Tempt
35. Soft drink variety
36. Hesitates
37. Put to sea
39. Establishment for brewing beer
40. Ashy substance
43. Young lion
45. Small isle
46. Choice steak (1-4)
47. Cylindrical larva
48. Forge worker
50. Primates
51. Misdeed
53. Gratuity
54. Top card
55. Piece
56. Drinking vessel

Puzzle 2

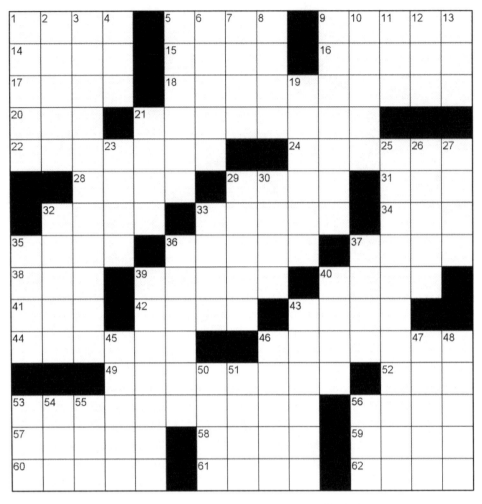

ACROSS
1. Highland skirt
5. Performs
9. Telephone
14. Ark builder
15. Natter
16. Hepatic organ
17. At one time
18. Combine with a halogen
20. Mouthpiece of a bridle
21. Boat having sails
22. Run hastily
24. Aver
28. Italian currency
29. Stubborn animal
31. Sea (French)
32. Skilfully
33. Authentic
34. Large snake
35. Hood-like membrane
36. The sesame plant
37. Clasp
38. Limb
39. Coniferous evergreen forest
40. Chill
41. Colorful form of the common carp
42. Australian super-model
43. Siamese
44. Group of nine
46. Twirl
49. Having no center
52. An age
53. Faultfinding
56. Former
57. Zodiac sign
58. Young guinea fowl
59. Ogle
60. Scapegoat
61. Hearing organs
62. Lazily

DOWN
1. Door handles
2. Grecian architectural style
3. Albumin of milk
4. Definite article
5. Ancient district in S Greece
6. Seat
7. Lofty
8. Post
9. Gratified
10. Clues
11. Eggs
12. Seine
13. Before
19. Goalkeeper
21. Agile
23. Grain factory
25. Decorated with ornamental needlework
26. Lubricate again
27. Snare
29. Skin disease of animals
30. Arm bone
32. Brother of Moses
33. Shroud
35. Shaped mass of food
36. Having less hair
37. Spur
39. Covering to keep a teapot hot (3-4)
40. Stylish
43. Winds together
45. Relaxes
46. More accurate
47. Scoundrel
48. Way in
50. Goddess of victory
51. New Guinea currency unit
53. Item of headwear
54. An age
55. Young louse
56. Biblical high priest

Puzzle 3

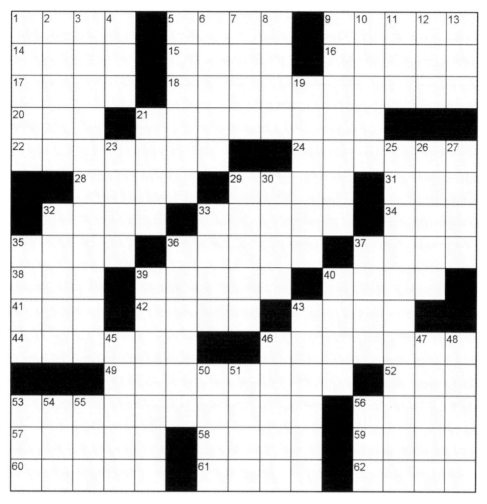

ACROSS
1. Resembling ink
5. Root of the taro
9. New Zealand aboriginal
14. African river
15. Performance by two
16. Downy duck
17. Monkeys
18. Intentional
20. Doze
21. Silicon compound
22. Manorial lands
24. Swindle
28. Is indebted
29. Portent
31. Cathedral city
32. Prayer ending
33. Fit new supports on chair
34. Automobile
35. Great quantity
36. Silent actor
37. Scene of first miracle
38. Long period of time
39. The base of a number system
40. Fiddling Roman emperor
41. Prefix, three
42. Sight organs
43. Point of hook
44. Leader of a revolt
46. Agitate
49. Liveliness
52. Fish eggs
53. Discerning
56. Delineate
57. Wan
58. Poker stake
59. Islamic call to prayer
60. Fern seed
61. Scent
62. Refuse

DOWN
1. Vapid
2. East Indies palms
3. Compulsion to steal
4. Affirmative response
5. Whirlpools
6. Grudge fights
7. Delicatessen
8. Auricular
9. Assembling
10. Ventilated
11. Room within a harem
12. Soak flax
13. Anger
19. Torment
21. Submachine gun
23. Overwhelmed
25. Remove carbon from
26. Grassy plain
27. Jaguarundi
29. Lead ups to finals
30. Holly
32. Oak nut
33. Travel on
35. Bristle
36. Perhaps
37. Certainty (Colloq)
39. Lie back
40. Never
43. Preferable
45. Sprinter
46. Piebald
47. Latin
48. Amphetamine tablet
50. Goodbye
51. Tear
53. Dance step
54. Extrasensory perception
55. 17th letter of the Greek alphabet
56. Boy

Puzzle 4

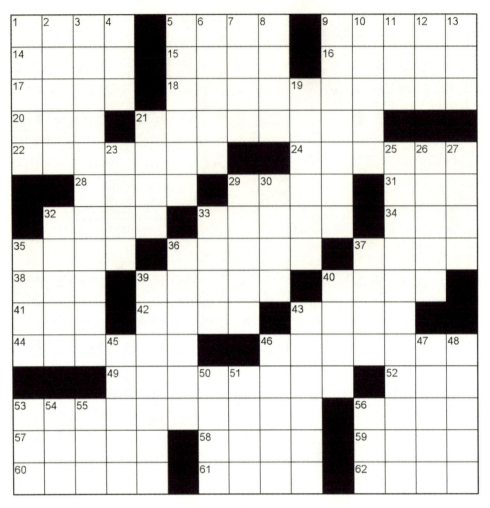

ACROSS
1. Skating area
5. Sloping walkway
9. More wily
14. Sewing case
15. To the sheltered side
16. Depart
17. Inhabitant of a Baltic state
18. With bare legs
20. Former measure of length
21. Irrigating
22. Salt of cyanic acid
24. Sacred shrine
28. Western pact
29. Row
31. Greek letter
32. Stop
33. Leper
34. Zero
35. Large bay
36. Crypts
37. Cotton seed vessel
38. Lubricant
39. Silk cotton
40. Drill
41. An age
42. Desires
43. Massive wild ox
44. Do a resection on
46. Cougar
49. Railway ties
52. Black bird
53. Cleansing
56. Upswept hairdo
57. Prickly plant
58. Hereditary factor
59. Closed
60. Tote
61. Mast
62. Sight organs

DOWN
1. Renaissance fiddle
2. Mediterranean country
3. Aboriginal clubs (5-6)
4. Pack
5. Wide stiff collar
6. Winged
7. Lake
8. Equal
9. Thin
10. Long-legged
11. Synthetic yttrium aluminum garnet
12. First woman
13. Colour
19. Climbing plants
21. Power unit
23. Naive person
25. Suture of a tendon
26. Useful
27. Shopping centre
29. Young sheep
30. Log house of rural Russia
32. Paper quantity
33. Meat cut
35. Apparently successful project
36. Sway
37. Boxing contest
39. Shop that sells bicycles
40. Prohibits
43. Leg band worn to keep up stocking
45. Chemical compound
46. Contour feather
47. Invest
48. Uproars
50. Ova
51. Furtive look
53. Government broadcaster
54. Brassiere
55. Knight's title
56. Avail of

Puzzle 5

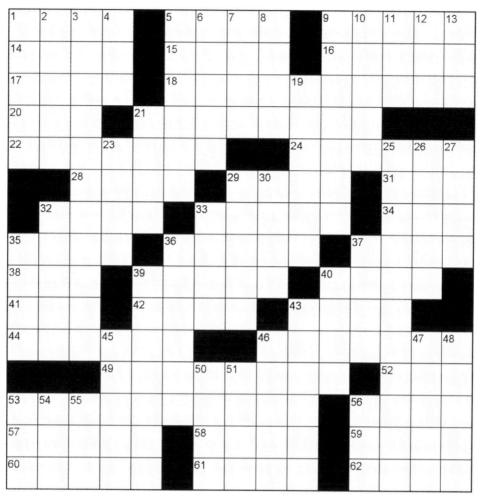

ACROSS
1. In due manner
5. Authentic
9. Level
14. Tennis star, - Natase
15. Photograph of bones (1-3)
16. Hot dish
17. Candid
18. Fatness
20. Father
21. Restoration
22. Foes
24. Made of silk
28. Crucifix
29. Primordial giant in Norse myth
31. Revised form of Esperanto
32. Card game
33. Items of currency
34. Monetary unit of Romania
35. Scandinavian Fate
36. Brass wind instrument
37. Helsinki citizen
38. Highest mountain in Crete
39. - and credit
40. Intentions
41. Relation
42. Periods of history
43. Jaguarundi
44. Inflammatory condition of the skin
46. Person to whom property is transferred
49. Member of a Rotary Club
52. Black
53. Expert in strategy
56. Mend socks
57. Angry
58. Australian super-model
59. Melody
60. Church council
61. Marsh plant
62. Sorrows

DOWN
1. Electrical rectifier
2. Hebrew school
3. Soft cheese
4. Japanese currency
5. Surpass
6. Crucifix
7. Male deer
8. Typographical error
9. Chocolate and cream delicacies
10. Subdue
11. Vase
12. Part of a circle
13. Soap ingredient
19. Bearlike
21. Uproar
23. Groan
25. Highest peak in Africa
26. Paradises
27. Proper word
29. Practitioners of yoga
30. Spleen
32. Containing sodium
33. Republic in the Caribbean
35. Goddess of victory
36. Chide
37. Flame
39. Lowered in rank
40. 16th letter of the Hebrew alphabet
43. Overjoyed
45. Muse of poetry
46. Church walkway
47. Weird
48. Alcohol burners
50. Maturing agent
51. Anger
53. Sister
54. Attempt
55. Fled
56. Black bird

Puzzle 6

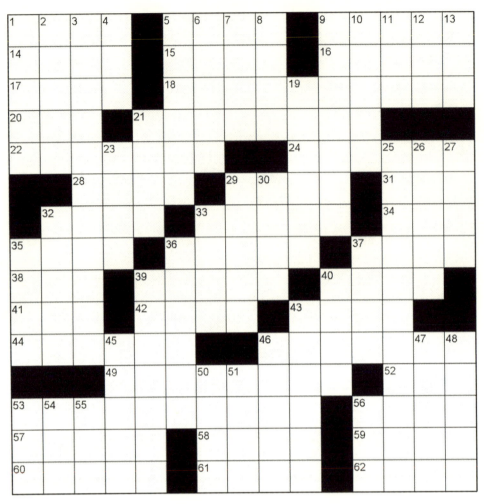

ACROSS
1. 8th letter of the Hebrew alphabet
5. Burden
9. Indian princess
14. Australian explorer
15. Sinister
16. Prefix, wind
17. Radiograph
18. Of great volume
20. Assist
21. An amorous glance
22. Condescended
24. The right side
28. Pedal digits
29. Old injury mark
31. Cheer
32. Person who lies
33. Confidence tricks
34. Crude mineral
35. Nourishment
36. Large duck-like bird
37. Hawaiian dance
38. Sea eagle
39. Add again
40. Tasks
41. Light meal
42. Current month
43. Lofty
44. Entwine
46. Sowers of seed
49. Artillery fragments
52. Saturate
53. A restriction
56. Measure of medicine
57. Avoid
58. Literary work
59. So be it
60. More modern
61. Compassion
62. For fear that

DOWN
1. Group of six
2. Eagle's nest
3. According to lore
4. Attention-getting call
5. Flood embankments
6. Evade
7. Pickling herb
8. 12th month of the Jewish calendar
9. Marauders
10. Append
11. Prefix, new
12. Australian bird
13. Greek goddess of the dawn
19. Title for a woman
21. Unique thing
23. Spur
25. Bothersome
26. Noblemen
27. Ostrichlike bird
29. Dart off
30. Mould
32. Actress, Sophia -
33. Drunkards
35. Bazaar
36. Species
37. Clasp
39. Earthquake scale
40. Woman who killed Sisera
43. Tiny
45. Stage whisper
46. Nose
47. Fragrant flowers
48. Outlaid
50. At the apex
51. Small mollusc
53. Pet form of Leonard
54. I have
55. Stomach
56. Indian dish

Puzzle 7

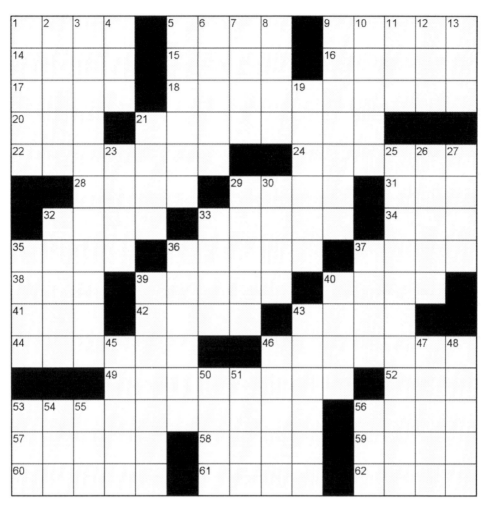

ACROSS
1. Immature flowers
5. Peaks
9. Neckcloth
14. Single entity
15. Monetary unit of Iran
16. Of the poles
17. June 6, 1944
18. Bad handwriting
20. Congeal
21. Artillery fragments
22. Built
24. Artists' stands
28. Dressed
29. Fetid
31. Pinch
32. Agitate
33. Crucifix
34. French vineyard
35. French fry
36. Hips
37. Type of jazz
38. Part of a circle
39. Lake in the Sierra Nevada
40. Twosomes
41. An infusion
42. English public school
43. Wind instrument
44. Resembling an owl
46. Chooses
49. Furtive
52. A dynasty in China
53. Ursa Minor
56. Limousine (Colloq)
57. Love affair
58. Molten rock
59. Unique thing
60. Sand hills
61. Paradise
62. Monster

DOWN
1. Move
2. Below
3. Pert. to dialectics
4. Pig enclosure
5. Having the form of an arch
6. River in W Canada
7. Large almost tailless rodent
8. Splash
9. Expands
10. Embers
11. High mountain
12. Cheer
13. Cook in oil
19. Metamorphic rock
21. Leading player
23. Fastener
25. Advancing beyond proper limits
26. Italian monies
27. Potato (Colloq)
29. The Hunter
30. Solitary
32. Termagant
33. Small salmon
35. Roman censor
36. Froth
37. Pipe
39. Bed canopies
40. In due manner
43. Capital of Iran
45. Hand out
46. Staff (Music)
47. Less feral
48. Sleeping noise
50. Capable
51. Heavy metal
53. Chield
54. Australian bird
55. Male offspring
56. Forfeit or sum paid into the pool

Puzzle 8

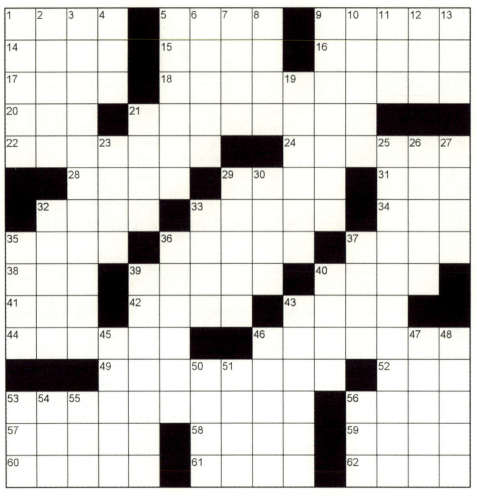

ACROSS
1. Heat, sweeten, and spice wine
5. Pain
9. Of the cheek
14. Eye part
15. Minor oath
16. Stadium
17. Require
18. Gentleman's evening dress (6.4)
20. Rum
21. Cowboy
22. Male roe deer
24. Voiced
28. Network of nerves
29. Grain husk
31. Dove's call
32. Card game
33. Surfeits
34. Gear wheel
35. Australian racehorse trainer, - Cummings
36. Monetary unit of Poland
37. Moat
38. 7th letter of the Greek alphabet
39. Free of ice
40. Ireland
41. Son of Jacob
42. Finishes
43. Marsh plant
44. Substance that causes a chemical reaction
46. Salt sulfurous acid
49. Weirdness
52. Egg drink
53. Agents
56. Maturing agent
57. Water-repellent cloth
58. Pinnacle
59. Blue-gray
60. Slack
61. Nidus
62. Wen

DOWN
1. Lesser
2. Hives
3. Soft cheese
4. Hallucinogenic drug
5. Cite
6. Spasmodic cramp
7. Skein
8. Sicilian volcano
9. Leaves stranded
10. Illegal burning
11. Monetary unit of Romania
12. Black bird
13. Rodent
19. As a substitute
21. Stub
23. Vanquish
25. Therefore
26. Snare
27. Swimsuits
29. Political combines
30. Stratagem
32. The Devil
33. Network
35. English monk
36. Species
37. Fee
39. Domain
40. Long fish
43. Reddish brown
45. Agreements
46. Appears
47. New Guinea currency units
48. Wading bird
50. Republic in SW Asia
51. Pleasing
53. Former measure of length
54. Cattle low
55. Revised form of Esperanto
56. Government broadcaster

Puzzle 9

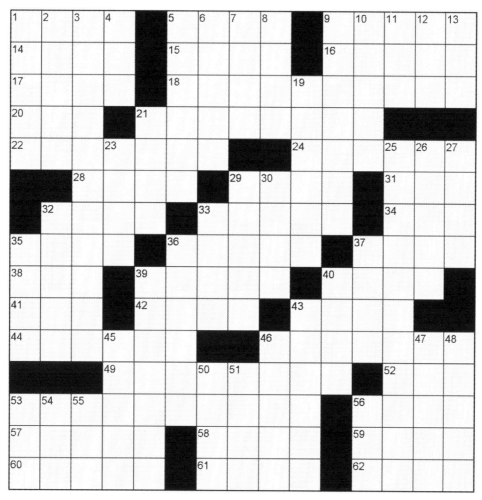

ACROSS
1. Back
5. Taxis
9. Dye
14. Extent of space
15. Gemstone
16. Climb
17. Final
18. Laudatory
20. Superlative suffix
21. Pique
22. Burst open
24. Whipped
28. Sea eagle
29. Weight allowance
31. Mount - , N.W. Qld. mining town
32. Springing gait
33. Climbing vine
34. Ethnic telecaster
35. Adherent of Jainism
36. Vampire
37. Egyptian deity
38. Curve
39. Cooked in oven
40. Diving bird
41. By way of
42. Frozen confections
43. Dull person
44. Sloping
46. Established
49. Imposing buildings
52. Brown-capped boletus mushroom
53. Patrician rank
56. Prima donna
57. Encore
58. Old
59. Auricular
60. Beseech again
61. Small children
62. Wen

DOWN
1. Breathed rattlingly
2. Rub out
3. Relating to aesthetics
4. Rodent
5. Compel
6. Venezuelan river
7. Indonesian resort island
8. Narrow opening
9. Mimic
10. Jewish lawgiver
11. However
12. Prefix, one
13. Etcetera
19. Principal ore of lead
21. Is not
23. Press clothes
25. Historical authenticity
26. Convocation of witches
27. Sprint
29. Occasions
30. Incursion
32. Hindu garments
33. Tarn
35. Main island of Indonesia
36. Pertaining to milk
37. Pond
39. Restrictive
40. Food fish
43. Loses blood
45. Eagle's nest
46. Group of eight
47. One of the Leeward Islands
48. Moon age at start of year
50. Decree
51. The villain in Othello
53. Normal
54. Mature
55. Label
56. Doctor

Puzzle 10

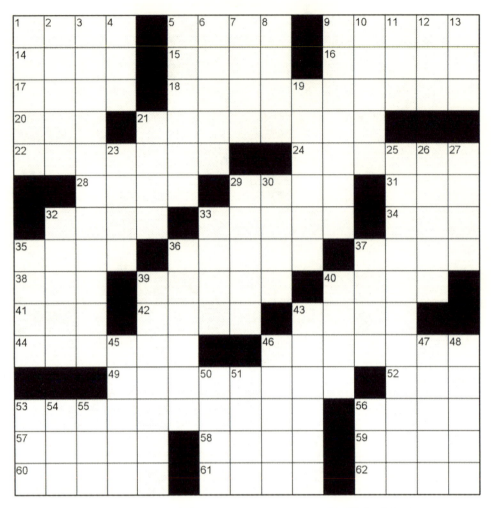

ACROSS
1. City-dweller holidaying on a ranch
5. Knot in wool
9. Fragrant oil
14. Capital of Western Samoa
15. At sea
16. Merrily
17. Former Soviet Union
18. Lawful
20. Unit of loudness
21. Speak at length
22. Stars (Heraldry)
24. Malay garment
28. Raccoon
29. Thin fog
31. Turkish governor
32. Stick used by a magician
33. Person hiring
34. Lavatory (Colloq)
35. Food scraps
36. Dromedary
37. Father
38. Colorful form of the common carp
39. Jabs
40. Cooking implements
41. Tavern
42. Regretted
43. Relax
44. Milk and egg drink
46. Goods sent from a country
49. Tranquillity
52. Exclamation of surprise
53. Travellers
56. Pace
57. Soft drinks
58. Public disturbance
59. Prefix, air
60. Excrete
61. Old cloth measures
62. River in central Europe

DOWN
1. Meat stew braised in red wine
2. Make unhappy
3. Displacing
4. Otic organ
5. Whalebone
6. Consumers
7. Car registration (Colloq)
8. Den
9. Stir
10. Less feral
11. - Maria, coffee liqueur
12. High-pitched
13. Cereal
19. Ornamental pendant consisting of a bunch of loose threads
21. Walk wearily
23. Charged particles
25. Effaced
26. Approaches
27. Fetter
29. Acted silently
30. Angers
32. Incorrect
33. Codlike fish
35. Migrant farm worker
36. Puma
37. Just passable (2-2)
39. Voice discontent
40. Father
43. Lives
45. Grandmothers
46. Laud
47. That place
48. Flavor
50. Uncommon
51. Indigo
53. Freeze
54. To clothe
55. Island (France)
56. Cracker biscuit

12

Puzzle 11

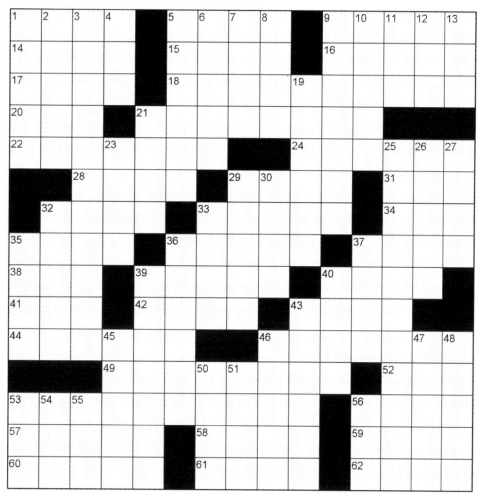

ACROSS
1. Portend
5. Sweet potatoes
9. Bundle of sticks
14. Days before
15. Confess
16. Two islands in the N Bahamas
17. Frighten
18. Systematic description of diseases
20. Dined
21. Study of human settlements
22. Nullified
24. Insect
28. Ritual
29. Indian ox
31. Even (poet.)
32. Yield
33. Antic
34. Lavatory (Colloq)
35. Wise
36. Teller
37. Repudiate
38. Wood sorrel
39. A parent
40. Coxae
41. Buddhist temple
42. Charge over property
43. Never
44. Originating in the mind
46. Prolific
49. Mechanic's garments
52. Singer, - "King" Cole
53. Hard to please
56. Engrave with acid
57. Gray
58. Upon
59. The power to reject
60. Poem
61. Adolescent
62. Greek god of love

DOWN
1. Commenced
2. Egg-shaped
3. Eliminate segregation
4. Superlative suffix
5. Federal soldier in the Civil War
6. Evade
7. Lichen
8. Study
9. Joker
10. Humiliate
11. Hiatus
12. Scottish expression
13. Plaything
19. Speak foolishly
21. Suffix, diminutive
23. Assistant
25. Teletypewriter
26. Slants
27. Jealousy
29. 7th letter of the Hebrew alphabet
30. Fencing sword
32. Chocolate nut
33. Juniper
35. Seeded
36. Carved
37. Food regimen
39. Green gem
40. Belonging to that woman
43. Trafalgar hero
45. Indian idol
46. Wind instrument
47. Prefix, milk
48. Spirit
50. Uproar
51. First class (1-3)
53. Distant
54. Fire remains
55. Timid
56. First woman

Puzzle 12

ACROSS
1. River deposit
5. Duration
9. Paces
14. Forest growth
15. Item of merchandise
16. Stop
17. Rant
18. Ether
20. Consumed
21. Exclusion
22. Of the oceans
24. Clover
28. Colours
29. Prefix, beyond
31. Chatter
32. Prefix, well
33. Prohibit
34. Monetary unit of Burma
35. Decree
36. Hereditary factors
37. Necklace component
38. Aged
39. Secreting organ
40. Eating implement
41. Period of human life
42. Indian queen
43. Nipple
44. Account book
46. One who questions
49. Hemmed in by ice
52. And not
53. Regarded
56. Measure out
57. Smell
58. The maple
59. Rectangular pier
60. Wood joint
61. Japanese syllabic script
62. Springing gait

DOWN
1. Leather strip
2. Angry
3. Sensible
4. Golf peg
5. Hindu religious teachers
6. Stampede
7. Greek god of war
8. Scottish headland
9. Student
10. Adolescent years
11. Consume
12. Pressure symbol
13. Dry (wine)
19. Coronets
21. Double curve
23. Female relative
25. Rude
26. Eskimo boat
27. Minor oath
29. Monetary unit of Finland
30. In bed
32. Ship bottom
33. University head
35. Young horse
36. Looked piercingly at
37. Hog
39. Greek
40. Give food to
43. Arcric plain
45. Gadget
46. Monarch
47. - voce, in a low tone
48. Behave towards
50. Bill
51. Killer whale
53. Small domesticated carnivore
54. Crude mineral
55. Prefix, not
56. Mothers

Puzzle 13

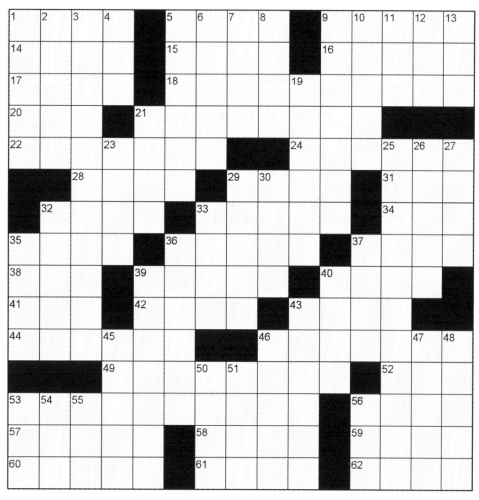

ACROSS
1. Prefix, foreign
5. Swedish pop-group of the '70s
9. Nautical, to the left
14. Always
15. Pacific island U.S. naval base
16. Perchlike game fish
17. Strike forcefully
18. Lawsuit
20. Sin
21. Accursed
22. Resembling a cyst
24. Rebelled
28. Jot
29. The sacred scriptures of Hinduism
31. Of us
32. Barbarous person
33. Ruses
34. In favor of
35. Continuous dull pain
36. Tobacco product
37. Broth
38. Prefix, whale
39. - Welles, actor, producer, and director
40. Canines
41. Actress, - West
42. Slew
43. Bindi-eye prickle
44. Invested
46. Leaping
49. Befitting clergymen
52. "The Raven" author
53. Represented in tapestry
56. Spacing wedge
57. Solo
58. Strong wind
59. Assist
60. Move smoothly
61. - Khayyam
62. Formerly

DOWN
1. Mediterranean vessel
2. All
3. Myopic (4-7)
4. Food scrap
5. One of the Graces
6. Construct
7. Restrain
8. Among
9. Wattle trees
10. African loris
11. Japanese sash
12. - de Janeiro
13. Brown shade
19. Steel beam
21. Dust speck
23. Ripped
25. Specialist in topography
26. The east wind
27. Let fall
29. Vitality
30. Dash
32. Large body of water
33. Sensible
35. Peak
36. Debit and -
37. Classify
39. Superintend
40. Punctually
43. Having less hair
45. Turn upside down (2-3)
46. Gravestone
47. Wool fibres
48. Seduce
50. Therefore
51. Thailand
53. Label
54. Everything
55. Hawaiian food
56. That woman

Puzzle 14

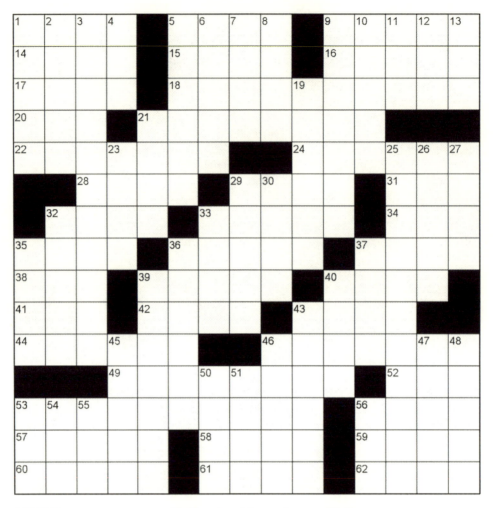

ACROSS
1. Type of automatic gear selector (1-3)
5. Gentle
9. Winged
14. Australian super-model
15. River in central Europe
16. Infectious
17. Bound
18. Courteous remark
20. Sixth scale note
21. An opening
22. Denied food to
24. Produced in pairs
28. Lure
29. Exchequer
31. Vex
32. Curve
33. Skirmish
34. Falsehood
35. Power unit
36. Distributed cards
37. Hotels
38. Biblical high priest
39. Fibbers
40. In this place
41. Turkish cap
42. Sea eagles
43. King mackerel
44. Sleeping sickness fly
46. Rushes in
49. Climbed
52. Comforter or quilt
53. Hygene goods
56. Deride
57. Elicit
58. Biting insect
59. Smart - , show-off
60. Unit of magnetic field strength
61. Sauce
62. Writing table

DOWN
1. Informs
2. Puff up
3. Arrange in alphabetical order
4. Female ruff
5. Young child
6. Lazed
7. Sly look
8. Damn
9. Greed
10. Napery
11. Illustrative craft
12. Road surfacing
13. Cathedral city
19. Set that is a part of a larger set
21. Eager
23. Rave
25. Person who likes cats
26. Clan
27. Supplements
29. Terrors
30. Evils
32. Wool packages
33. Intend
35. Warp and -. Weaving yarns
36. Straight
37. South American country
39. Persons renting
40. Flock of cattle
43. Plumes
45. Gossips
46. Notions
47. Progressive emaciation
48. Dot
50. Work units
51. One of Columbus's ships
53. Two-year old sheep
54. Eggs
55. Acknowledgement of debt
56. Goad for driving cattle

Puzzle 15

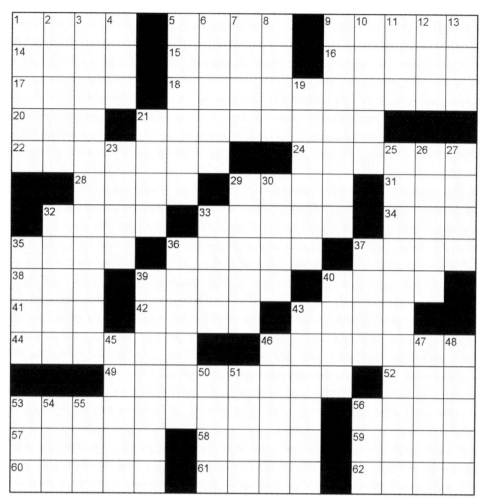

ACROSS
1. Heraldry, wide horizontal stripe on shield
5. Reverberate
9. Solidly fix in surrounding mass
14. Notion
15. Anchor vessel
16. Pale bluish purple
17. Combining form meaning " strange "
18. The wood of ebony trees
20. Printer's measures
21. Irking
22. Flowers
24. Fairy
28. Bread rolls
29. Foolish
31. An age
32. Act silently
33. Indian currency
34. Long-leaved lettuce
35. Insect feeler
36. Stripped
37. First-class
38. Israeli submachine gun
39. Bindi-eye prickles
40. Possesses
41. Greeted
42. Region
43. Raced
44. Nosy
46. Shabbier
49. Assisting the memory
52. Prefix, three
53. Desperate criminals
56. Public disturbance
57. Higher
58. Standard
59. Rubber pipe
60. Faces
61. Non-scientific studies
62. Single items

DOWN
1. Repaired
2. Dropsy
3. Capacity for feeling
4. Cracker biscuit
5. Masters of ceremonies
6. Outer garments
7. Former Australian P.M. Harold -
8. Spoken
9. Issue
10. Skin disease of animals
11. Immature flower
12. Day before
13. The (German)
19. Ticked
21. Number of Muses
23. Cesspool
25. Restore to good state
26. Presses clothes
27. Relax
29. Indian millet
30. Primates
32. Large drinking bowl
33. Uncommon
35. Inflating tool
36. Bun with meat etc.
37. Impressed
39. Flags
40. Oil cartel
43. Earthquakes
45. Force forward
46. Grunt
47. Uneven
48. Rituals
50. Supernatural power
51. Scent
53. A failure
54. Prefix, over
55. Mineral spring
56. 17th letter of the Greek alphabet

Puzzle 16

ACROSS
1. Responsibility
5. Plan
9. Slumber
14. Air duct opening
15. A corpse
16. Cuban ballroom dance
17. Askew
18. Predecessor
20. Sheltered side
21. Person-to-person
22. Make less taut
24. Ice cream made with eggs
28. Matching outfit
29. One who is indebted
31. Beetle
32. Be defeated
33. Thorny
34. Change colour of
35. Scottish hills
36. Perfume
37. Reared
38. Garland
39. A heap
40. - off, began golf game
41. Sea eagle
42. Charity
43. Crude minerals
44. Past
46. Backer
49. Owned to
52. Monkey
53. Violent disagreement
56. Funeral notice
57. Shakespearian sprite
58. Lazy
59. Bone of the forearm
60. Altar stone
61. Pip
62. Profound

DOWN
1. Sportsgrounds
2. Stair post
3. Irrational
4. Pigpen
5. Mars or Venus
6. Fabric woven from flax yarns
7. Prefix, eight
8. At that time
9. Landscape
10. Scoundrel
11. Abstract being
12. The self
13. Normal
19. Believable
21. Migrant farm worker
23. Curse
25. Capable of being addressed
26. Flirted
27. Angered
29. Unseals
30. Breeze
32. Wary
33. Offscourings
35. A bubble
36. Grave
37. "Has - ". Person who once was
39. Antiapartheid activist
40. Walked
43. Unlocked
45. Fertile desert spots
46. Fur wrap
47. Think
48. Rap with fingers again
50. Egyptian goddess of fertility
51. Ocean fluctuation
53. Weir
54. Wrath
55. Transgress
56. Musical instrument

Puzzle 17

ACROSS
1. Chest
5. Skills
9. Make amends
14. Dame - Everage, Humphries' character
15. Monetary unit of Iran
16. Sum up
17. Sound of a cat
18. Persons who claim superior enlightenment
20. Average
21. Convert to Islam
22. Sleeping sickness flies
24. Drunken
28. Cut of meat
29. Boatswain
31. Attention-getting call
32. Unlocking implements
33. Capital of Crete
34. Sea eagle
35. Employer
36. Stripped
37. French cheese
38. - Vegas, US gambling city
39. Toboggans
40. Cupola
41. Everything
42. Swellings
43. Mother of Apollo
44. Hay stored in a barn
46. Column in the form of a man
49. Legal status of an alien
52. Female sheep
53. Permeate
56. Inflammation (Suffix)
57. Monetary unit of Sierra Leone
58. Candid
59. Hire
60. Actress, Sophia -
61. Reddish brown chalcedony
62. Work units

DOWN
1. Tidily kept
2. Notions
3. Sleeping silently
4. Choice marble
5. Cropped up
6. Rivulets
7. Monetary unit of Western Samoa
8. Squalid city area
9. State in SW United States
10. Belief
11. Wood sorrel
12. Singer, - "King" Cole
13. Prefix, over
19. Failed to hit
21. Egyptian goddess of fertility
23. Playthings
25. Temperature measuring instrument
26. Strange and mysterious
27. Unit of force
29. Poets
30. Singles
32. Australian marsupial
33. City in NW France
35. Meaningless chatter
36. Edible pale-bluish mushroom
37. Goatskin bag for holding wine
39. Tumid
40. Delete (Printing)
43. Myth
45. US State
46. Potato (Colloq)
47. Unpaid
48. Nidi
50. Greek god of love
51. Soft lambskin leather
53. Sick
54. Prefix, new
55. In favour of
56. Wrath

Puzzle 18

ACROSS
1. Restrain
5. Garden tool
9. Loincloth worn by Hindu men
14. Fertiliser
15. Absent
16. Ranted
17. Having wealth
18. Territory under a palatine
20. Metal rod
21. Insurrection
22. Bombarded
24. Tending to skid
28. First-class
29. Continuous dull pain
31. Crude mineral
32. Portico
33. Beatles' drummer, Ringo -
34. Witty remark
35. Move in water
36. Small yeast-raised pancake
37. Prefix, part
38. Also
39. Loops
40. Undergo lysis
41. Over there
42. Ecstatic
43. Wife of one's uncle
44. Follows
46. Icy
49. Capital of Nepal
52. Dove sound
53. Diplomatic official
56. Point of hook
57. Farm bird
58. Animistic god or spirit
59. Suffix, diminutive
60. Possessed
61. Portent
62. Deceased

DOWN
1. Restrains
2. - Heep, Dickens character
3. Pastimes
4. Expression of contempt
5. Strong snuff
6. Bestow
7. Wife of Shiva
8. Nestling
9. Tippler
10. Maori feast
11. Eggs
12. 9th letter of the Hebrew alphabet
13. Carp-like fish
19. First month of the Jewish calendar
21. Arm bone
23. Appear threateningly
25. Tame
26. Aircraft field
27. Abominable snowman
29. Leaning
30. Tins
32. Faint
33. Slide
35. Eye inflammation
36. Brags
37. Synchronize
39. Wrinkled
40. Hawaiian feast
43. Second man on the moon
45. Edict of the czar
46. Goblin
47. Major artery
48. Having lobes
50. Mackerel shark
51. First man
53. In the past
54. Cut lawn
55. French, good
56. Cot

Puzzle 19

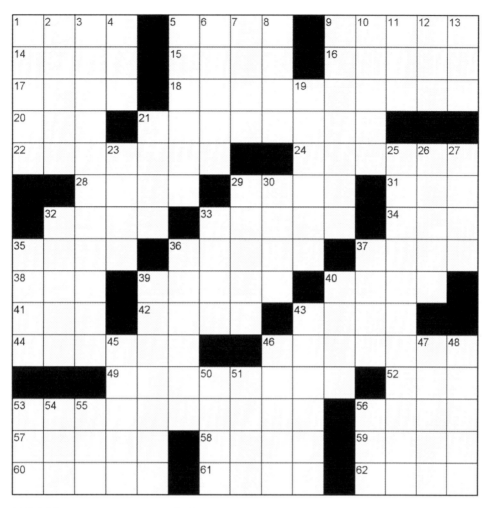

ACROSS
1. Beancurd
5. Blackjack
9. Alcohol burners
14. Greek goddess of the rainbow
15. Opera solo
16. Small violin
17. Monetary unit of Italy
18. Reallocated
20. Scottish river
21. Panicked rush
22. Jostled
24. Small leaping rodent
28. Monetary unit of Iran
29. South American bird
31. Greeting
32. Dairy product
33. Contraction of has not
34. Card game
35. Droops
36. Reassembled
37. Reclined
38. - Maria, coffee liqueur
39. Sides
40. Arm extremity
41. Eccentric
42. Indolently
43. Secular
44. Spurious
46. Tiaras
49. Wine variety
52. Bleat of a sheep
53. Sixty
56. Cult
57. Forest
58. At sea
59. Wife of Shiva
60. Monastery head
61. Blackbird
62. Prayer ending

DOWN
1. Diacritic
2. Bay window
3. Group of firefighters
4. North American nation
5. Trade association
6. Mountain nymph
7. Former name of Thailand
8. Lock part fitted to staple
9. Obvious
10. Large cat
11. Not (prefix)
12. Beer
13. Morose
19. Sitting
21. Sealed with a kiss
23. Lubricates
25. Gymnastic event for women
26. Egg-shaped
27. Great age
29. Lame
30. Employs
32. Female servants
33. Cure
35. Halt
36. Repeats
37. Reposed
39. Neatest
40. Dutch name of The Hague
43. Of a direct ancestor
45. Hives
46. More dreadful
47. Twinned crystal
48. Glossy fabric
50. Confidence trick
51. Borne to be without
53. Two
54. Fireplace ledge
55. Hold up
56. Jamaican popular music

Puzzle 20

ACROSS
1. Pause
5. 6th month of the Jewish calendar
9. City in Nebraska
14. Paradise
15. Adult nits
16. More pleasant
17. Time of abstinence
18. Executives
20. - and outs, intricacies
21. Osteoid
22. Russian empress
24. Straight
28. Nurse
29. Portent
31. Sea (French)
32. Travel on
33. Bent
34. Filled pastry crust
35. Nourishment
36. French queen, - Antoinette
37. Fool
38. Flee
39. Models
40. The moon
41. Greek letter
42. Antarctic explorer
43. Wan
44. Bank cashier
46. Cake, wine, jam, custard and jelly desserts
49. Having no center
52. Fold
53. Regarded
56. Spanish words of agreement (2.2)
57. Zodiac sign
58. Neck hair
59. Unique thing
60. Length measure
61. Probability
62. Unattractive

DOWN
1. Rekindled
2. Paradises
3. Dramatic
4. An explosive
5. Nutlike kernel
6. Roman goddess of the moon
7. Adolescent pimples
8. True
9. A particular variety (3.4)
10. Silent actor
11. Top card
12. Female bird
13. Illustrative craft
19. Small Australian tree
21. Twining stem
23. Spawning area of salmon
25. Selecting jury
26. Silk cotton
27. Three (Cards)
29. Skin lesions
30. Certainly
32. Course
33. Freshwater fish
35. Worry
36. Anchored
37. Deep hollow
39. Exact
40. Secular
43. Groups of lions
45. Light beam
46. Tendency
47. Artist's support
48. Helical
50. Verne's submariner
51. Type of jazz
53. Eccentric shaft
54. Metal-bearing mineral
55. Young louse
56. Former coin of France

Puzzle 21

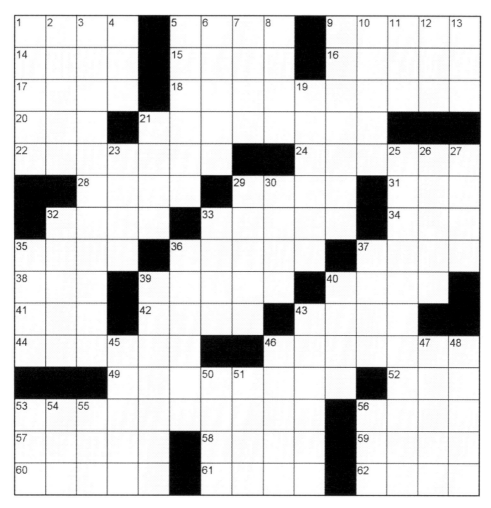

ACROSS
1. Strikes
5. Bear constellation
9. Musical drama
14. Image of a deity
15. Peruse
16. African antelope
17. Resembling vines
18. Newly married man
20. Greek goddess of the dawn
21. Wooden panel
22. Grinning
24. Snake sounds
28. Decoy
29. On top of
31. Monetary unit of Afghanistan
32. An alcoholic
33. German, war
34. Period of history
35. Tennis star, - Natase
36. Burn with water
37. Barge
38. Witty remark
39. Musty
40. Fly larvae
41. Greek letter
42. Friends
43. Frown
44. Broad ribbons
46. Study of rocks
49. Needle-shaped
52. New Guinea seaport
53. Mad dogs and these go out in the mid-day sun
56. Tells on
57. Depart
58. French clergyman
59. Leer
60. Deletion marks in printing
61. Having pedal digits
62. Sight organs

DOWN
1. Allergy rash
2. Jargon
3. Inflammation of the tonsils
4. Wily
5. Polite
6. Set up again
7. To bless
8. Increases
9. Continuing
10. Separates
11. Self-esteem
12. Kangaroo
13. Upper limb
19. Reverberated
21. Sinewy
23. One of the Disciples
25. The study of ghosts
26. Wallaroos
27. Cabbage salad
29. European mountains
30. Mound
32. Hawaiian farewell
33. Kilocalorie
35. Little devils
36. Stagnation
37. Inner spirit
39. Distinct sort or kind
40. Rude person
43. Tilted
45. Reduce to half
46. Soil
47. Architectural feature
48. Agreements
50. Converse
51. Boss on a shield
53. Antiquity
54. Born
55. Girl (Slang)
56. Female deer

Puzzle 22

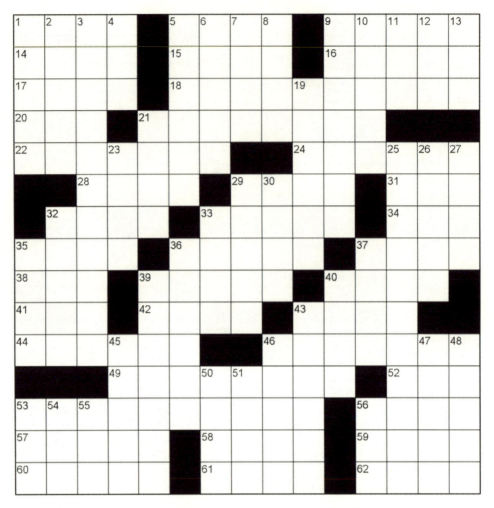

ACROSS
1. Woman who killed Sisera
5. Polynesian root food
9. Pass into disuse
14. Off-Broadway theater award
15. Ancient Greek coin
16. Similar
17. U.S. space agency
18. Pastry making tool (7.3)
20. Statute
21. Formerly Ceylon
22. German biologist
24. Blockades
28. Speaking platform
29. Festive occasion
31. An age
32. Appends
33. Navigational aid
34. Prefix, three
35. Flute
36. Polyp colony
37. Type of gun
38. Fuss
39. American witch hunt city
40. Timber
41. Last letter
42. Golf mounds
43. Encircle
44. Compositions
46. Station hands
49. Sideways
52. Decade
53. Wrestling hold
56. Siamese
57. Foreign
58. Migrant farm worker
59. Weal
60. Torment
61. Curve
62. 3 Weapons

DOWN
1. He lived in a whale
2. Manila hemp plant
3. Competitive music festivals
4. Meadow
5. Spanish navigator
6. Boiling
7. Trundle
8. Earthen pot
9. Taller and thinner
10. Pond scum
11. Fruit seed
12. Snow runner
13. Even (poet.)
19. Place in position
21. Snow runners
23. Juniper
25. Informal gathering
26. Went wrong
27. To bless
29. Transport ticket costs
30. Dutch cheese
32. Assistants
33. Part played
35. Fluster
36. Roman general
37. A carol
39. Common synthetic rubber
40. Grape beverage
43. Endangered
45. Pinnacles
46. Powder from castor-oil plant
47. Kingdom
48. Fits of rage
50. Jelly-like mass
51. Roused
53. Covering for the head
54. Beer
55. Actress, - Farrow
56. Two

Puzzle 23

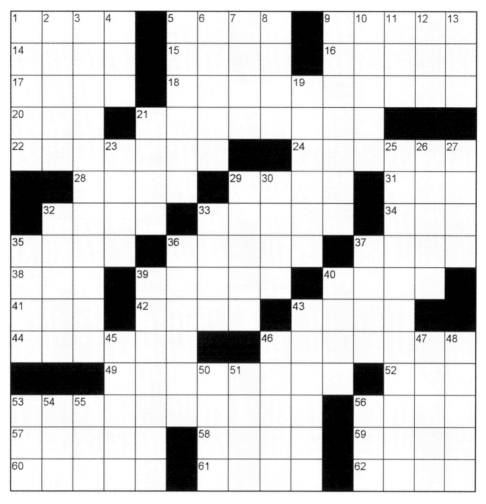

ACROSS
1. French novelist
5. Surreptitious, attention getting sound
9. Join
14. Baking chamber
15. Sicilian volcano
16. Lowest point
17. Tidy
18. Property
20. Bitter vetch
21. Air craft
22. Cowboy hat
24. Walk nonchalantly
28. Tilled
29. The maple
31. Yes
32. Soybean
33. Wattle species
34. Cooking implement
35. Old cloth measures
36. Appears
37. Skeletal part
38. Deity
39. Steeple
40. Drunkards
41. Open
42. Converts to leather
43. Heap
44. Watery
46. Punishment for sin
49. Reprimand
52. Uncle -, USA personified
53. Becoming milky
56. Movie
57. Wan
58. Prong
59. Trunk of a tree
60. Outlaid
61. Having wings
62. Current month

DOWN
1. Regions
2. Open
3. Tenant under a lease
4. Social insect
5. Length of time
6. Severe
7. Break suddenly
8. Lofty
9. Untangle
10. Buttocks
11. Highest mountain in Crete
12. Small bird
13. Before
19. Artists' stands
21. Seaward
23. Playthings
25. Decreased blood pressure
26. Ages
27. W.A. eucalypt
29. - Rock, Uluru
30. Arrived
32. Escarpment
33. Hitler's autobiography, "-Kampf"
35. Personalities
36. Fits
37. South American weapon
39. Scholar
40. Hyperbolic sine
43. Harass
45. Made of oats
46. Feather
47. Visits
48. Ant
50. Prefix, eight
51. - Armstrong, first man on moon
53. - Vegas, US gambling city
54. Egyptian serpent
55. - Guevara
56. Law enforcement agency

Puzzle 24

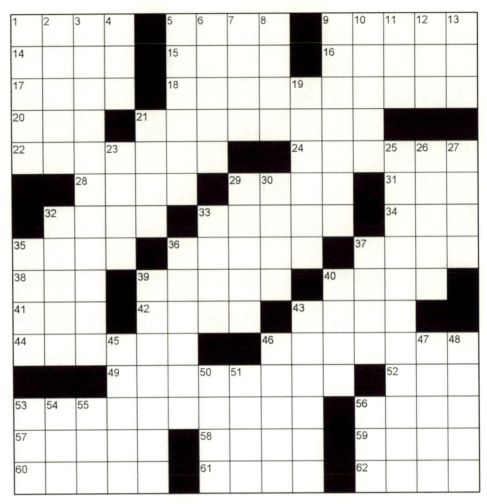

ACROSS
1. Midday
5. Pronoun
9. Nocturnal ungulate
14. Russian secret police
15. In this place
16. Small egg
17. Narrow aperture
18. Exculpated
20. Even (poet.)
21. Deserts
22. Bored
24. Glossy fabrics
28. Exclamation of mild dismay
29. Female servant
31. Louse egg
32. Taverns
33. Keyboard instrument
34. Born
35. Blue-gray
36. Public swimming pool
37. Air channel
38. High-pitched
39. Steps
40. Large volume
41. Hive insect
42. Having wings
43. Gaelic
44. Eager
46. Derided
49. Person's individual speech pattern
52. Atomic mass unit
53. Excision of part of the iris
56. French clergyman
57. Sprinter
58. Sacred Egyptian bird
59. Lath
60. Pitchers
61. Expense
62. Lock openers

DOWN
1. Nuzzled
2. Leerer
3. Dogmatic
4. Kernel
5. Ancient city in S Egypt
6. Group of six
7. Metallic element
8. Dispatch
9. Twister
10. Nautical cry
11. Place
12. Island (France)
13. Colour
19. Red dyes
21. Peaks
23. Solitary
25. Countless
26. Female relative
27. Let it stand
29. Headdress of a bishop
30. Exclamations of surprise
32. Sicker
33. Large almost tailless rodent
35. Small yeast cake
36. European sea
37. Prescribed amount
39. Caters to
40. Weight allowance
43. Enclose in a sac
45. Duck with soft down
46. Lead ups to finals
47. Surround
48. Performances by two
50. Auricular
51. American grey wolf
53. Anger
54. Uncooked
55. Frozen water
56. Inquire of

Puzzle 25

ACROSS
1. Metal band
5. Raced
9. Prehistoric chisellike tool
14. Dame - Everage, Humphries' character
15. Back of neck
16. Habituate
17. Bearing
18. Got rid of
20. Pressure symbol
21. Hawker
22. Striped
24. Renowned
28. Musical work
29. Coal dust
31. French vineyard
32. Prayer ending
33. Aromatic gum used in making incense
34. Eccentric wheel
35. Foretell
36. Seraglio
37. Cabins
38. Brown shade
39. Suffix, city
40. Item of merchandise
41. Killer whale
42. Rectangular pier
43. Tress
44. Abnormal
46. Guiltless
49. Embellished
52. Hard-shelled fruit
53. Authorized period of delay
56. Land measure
57. Draw forth
58. Earthen pot
59. Wax
60. Cavalry sword
61. Healthy
62. Russian emperor

DOWN
1. Fibrous plants
2. Writer of lyric poetry
3. Divination through dreams
4. Kitchen utensil
5. Moves stealthily
6. Chummy
7. Heroic
8. Demonstration
9. Below
10. Remove weapons from
11. Groove
12. Wrath
13. - Kelly
19. Tell
21. Woodland spirit
23. Fencing sword
25. Incidents
26. Salt of uric acid
27. Adds
29. Its capital is Damascus
30. Crude minerals
32. Asunder
33. Germinated grain
35. Portico
36. Bigshot
37. Greet
39. Artist
40. Baton
43. Wintry
45. Tranquillity
46. Row
47. Infectious blood disease
48. Direct
50. In a line
51. African river
53. My, French (Plural)
54. Room within a harem
55. Chafe
56. Play division

Puzzle 26

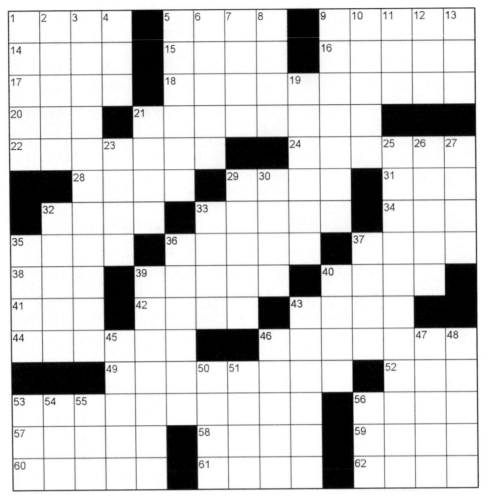

ACROSS
1. Transport ticket cost
5. Donations to the poor
9. - Heep, Dickens character
14. Fertiliser
15. Jump
16. Effeminate male
17. Back
18. Runner in a marathon
20. Annihilate
21. Nurtured
22. Marry
24. Christian festival
28. Kiln for drying hops
29. European race
31. Greek letter
32. Skills
33. High-toned
34. Drinking vessel
35. Consumes
36. Portents
37. To yield
38. Prefix, three
39. Braking chock
40. Uncommon
41. Also
42. Hastens
43. Information
44. Group of nine
46. Accounts
49. Mild laxative
52. Braggart (Colloq) (1.2)
53. Aboriginal instrument
56. At the bow of a vessel
57. Swiss song
58. Flutter
59. The moon
60. Entrance
61. Prefix, distant
62. Former Soviet Union

DOWN
1. Gorse
2. Regions
3. Distribute anew
4. Otic organ
5. Nearly
6. Rent agreement
7. Shopping centre
8. Foretell
9. Lift up
10. Land measures
11. Tavern
12. Very skilled person
13. That woman
19. Behaves towards
21. Bother
23. Cereal food
25. Reckless
26. Musical study piece
27. Storm
29. Heroic stories
30. Respiratory organ
32. Brother of Moses
33. Rent
35. Suffix, diminutive
36. Arachnid
37. Roman censor
39. Curvaceous
40. Ecstatic
43. Indicate
45. Keen
46. Lubricate again
47. Mountain lakes
48. Daub
50. Split
51. Doing nothing
53. Coloring material
54. Charged particle
55. Once common, now banned, insecticide
56. Influenza

Puzzle 27

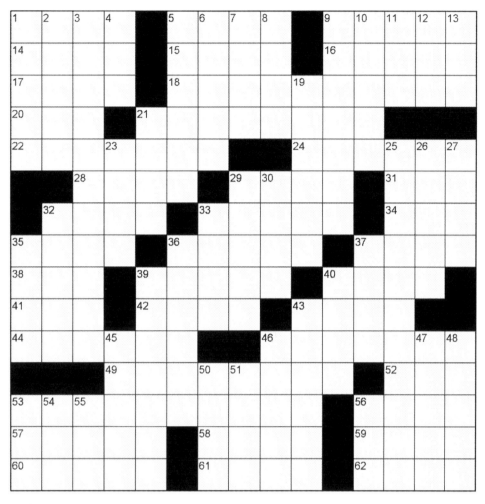

ACROSS
1. Routine
5. Wife of a rajah
9. Unseals
14. Supplements
15. Augury
16. Tell an untruth again
17. Inhabitant of a Baltic state
18. Italian sausage
20. Primate
21. Disable
22. The ropes, chains, sails, etc on a ship
24. Mouth (Slang)
28. Blushing
29. Scheme
31. Avail of
32. Chins
33. Smart - , show-offs
34. Pressure symbol
35. Delineate
36. Ember of the weasel family
37. Faculty head
38. Electrical resistance unit
39. Spacing wedges
40. Extremely
41. Not
42. Neck hair
43. Ring of bells
44. Swirled
46. Frame for hanging hats
49. Stately
52. Bind
53. Introspection
56. Nip
57. Lord
58. On sheltered side
59. Level
60. Waned
61. Pleased
62. Scottish headland

DOWN
1. Rod used to reinforce concrete
2. Giraffe-like animal
3. Wired
4. Superlative suffix
5. A Gipsy
6. Amid
7. Dweeb
8. Monetary unit of Peru
9. Confers holy orders upon
10. Furtive looks
11. Former measure of length
12. Naught
13. Large body of water
19. Antiaircraft fire
21. Snake sound
23. Robe
25. Of the highest order
26. Short story
27. Riding strap
29. Feather
30. Telescope part
32. Moslem holy war
33. Related
35. Solitary
36. Protected from sun
37. Expensive
39. Daubed
40. Override
43. Overtook
45. Icon
46. Hebrew prophet
47. Quotes
48. Wails
50. Catch
51. Inform
53. Island (France)
54. Pen point
55. Spider's structure
56. Scottish hill

Puzzle 28

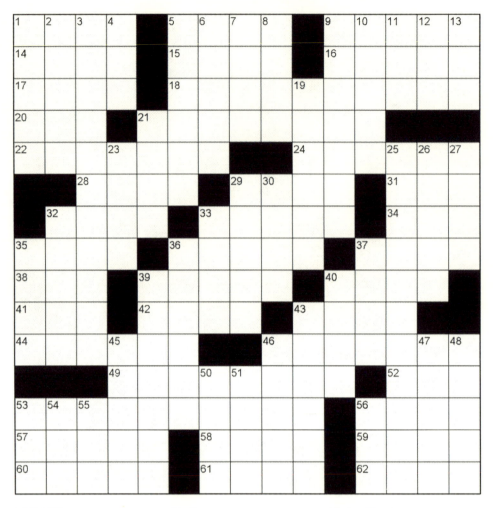

ACROSS
1. Blend
5. Grate
9. Fragrant resin
14. Woodman
15. 12th month of the Jewish calendar
16. Yucatan indian
17. Metropolis
18. Solitude
20. High-pitched
21. Cut a groove around tree trunk in order to kill it
22. Tearful
24. Ambush
28. Black bird
29. Handle of a knife
31. Australian bird
32. Fired a gun
33. Heavy stocking cap worn in Canada
34. Jelly
35. Never
36. African acacia tree
37. Twining stem
38. Eggs
39. Ballroom dance
40. Benevolent
41. Spread out for drying
42. Ruse
43. Lout
44. Follows
46. Monitor lizards
49. Sword sheathe
52. To be unwell
53. Frightening dreams
56. Prefix, thousand
57. More gelid
58. Anger
59. Developed
60. Prefix, four
61. Manager
62. Cots

DOWN
1. South American parrot
2. Banish
3. Stationery with printed heading
4. Arid
5. Reconnect
6. Lengthwise
7. Carolled
8. Plebeian
9. State of an emir
10. Tall and thin
11. Optic organ
12. Mothers
13. - and outs, intricacies
19. Legitimate
21. Uproar
23. Having no money
25. Member of French Foreign Legion
26. Alter
27. Christmas
29. Husband
30. Blue shade
32. Days in a week
33. Cap of Scottish origin
35. Musical symbol
36. Fragrant resin
37. Benefit
39. Ranges of colour
40. Spur
43. Equines
45. Escort in
46. Scots
47. Sickened
48. Reduces speed
50. Sharp bristle
51. Vigor
53. Louse egg
54. Frozen water
55. British, a fool
56. Soviet secret police

Puzzle 29

ACROSS
1. Knight's wife
5. Every
9. Brown pigment
14. Double curve
15. Chinese dynasty
16. Coniferous evergreen forest
17. Caution
18. The clergy
20. Prefix, over
21. Place where watercraft are stored
22. Keeps
24. Containing iridium
28. Look at amorously
29. First class (1-3)
31. An age
32. Genuine
33. Ceiled
34. Posed
35. A Great Lake
36. Blazes
37. Wagers
38. Cracker biscuit
39. Norsemen
40. Eat
41. Atomic mass unit
42. Second-hand
43. Without
44. Conclusion
46. Stuffing
49. Kitchen implements
52. Rocky peak
53. Fragrant S Asian grass
56. Peruvian capital
57. Greek theatre
58. Roman garment
59. As soon as possible
60. The sesame plant
61. Moved in water
62. English monk

DOWN
1. Endowment
2. With mouth wide open
3. Praiseworthy
4. Even (poet.)
5. Wager
6. Italian monies
7. Weave wool
8. Matures
9. Spoke
10. Muslim messiah
11. Prefix, life
12. The self
13. Radiation unit
19. Gleams
21. Gall
23. Malarial fever
25. Make less sensitive
26. Angry
27. Felines
29. Ventilated
30. Singles
32. Hobo
33. Row
35. Son of Isaac and Rebekah
36. Attach firmly
37. Tie
39. Printing in two colors
40. Fathers
43. Oriental greeting
45. A Great Lake
46. Small inland tree
47. Wanderer
48. Wine source
50. Devices for fishing
51. Sluggish
53. Corn ear
54. Carp-like fish
55. Decade
56. Laboratory

Puzzle 30

ACROSS
1. Tense
5. Expectorate
9. Fold
14. Russian secret police
15. Conceal
16. Vertical face of a stair
17. Time gone by
18. Voting district
20. 7th letter of the Greek alphabet
21. State of USA
22. Gives a new name
24. Nun
28. Trade agreement
29. Osculate
31. Cereal
32. Scent
33. Triad
34. Period of history
35. Press clothes
36. Plait
37. Surety
38. Novel
39. Profits
40. Sprint contest
41. Is able to
42. Charity
43. Speed relative to the speed of sound
44. Superficially absorb
46. Scent bags
49. Snobbish conduct
52. Female ruff
53. Hiding
56. Cajole
57. Anigh
58. Against
59. Trick
60. Dull people
61. Paradise
62. Employs

DOWN
1. Heavy drinker
2. Gemstone
3. Good and bad times
4. Minor admonishment
5. Monetary unit of Israel
6. Tablets
7. Notion
8. Technical college (Colloq)
9. Vow
10. Italian monies
11. Mount - , N.W. Qld. mining town
12. Prefix, whale
13. Land measure
19. Threw
21. - Khayyam
23. Great age
25. Disloyal
26. Eagle's nest
27. Genuine
29. Persian lords
30. Eye part
32. Mountain nymph
33. Decorate (Xmas tree)
35. South American Indian
36. Monetary unit of Panama
37. German composer
39. Gleans
40. Risque
43. Border
45. Academy Award
46. Monetary unit of Lesotho
47. Torment
48. Genders
50. Blue-gray
51. To bandage
53. Taxi
54. Yoko -
55. Prefix, new
56. French vineyard

Puzzle 31

ACROSS
1. Lad
6. Repast
11. Island (France)
14. Suspension of breathing
15. Navigational aid
16. Soldiers
17. Of necessity
19. Seed vessel
20. Nautical mile
21. Eskimo dwelling
22. Hereditary factor
23. Always
25. Daubed
27. Short lyric poem
31. Supplements
32. Affirmative vote
33. Voltage regulating semiconductor diode
35. Run off
38. Agreement
40. Dart off
42. Scorning person
43. Brief
45. Follow
47. Long-sleeved linen vestment
48. Skin
50. Comestibles
52. Article of personal property
55. Heart
56. Routine
57. Purvey
59. Appendage
63. Prefix, one
64. Crust of the earth
66. Spanish title
67. Farewell
68. Strange and mysterious
69. Unit of energy
70. Hereditary factors
71. Sheen

DOWN
1. Tug
2. Candid
3. Remarkable
4. Sway
5. Owns
6. Perfume
7. British nobleman
8. Farewell
9. Biblical dancing girl
10. Attempt
11. Lacking human emotion
12. Monetary unit of Sierra Leone
13. Finished
18. Blockades
22. Scots
24. Videlicet
26. Supplement
27. Charts
28. Indian nursemaid
29. Adorning
30. Monetary unit of Sierra Leone
34. Rosy
36. Mast
37. Wanes
39. Banal
41. Instructs
44. An explosive
46. Organ of hearing
49. Determine
51. Sanctuary
52. Unrefined
53. High public esteem
54. Roman
58. You
60. Air (prefix)
61. Greek goddess of the rainbow
62. Dregs
64. A delay
65. Wooden pin

Puzzle 32

ACROSS
1. Language spoken in S China
6. Turkish governor
11. - and don'ts
14. An occasion
15. Man's race
16. Questioning exclamation
17. Of necessity
19. Dined
20. Streetcar
21. Muse of poetry
22. Immense
23. Hawaiian honeycreeper
25. Phantom
27. Confusing language of the legal profession
31. Russian parliament before 1917
32. Lubricant
33. Sauerkraut
35. Started
38. Spoken
40. Fathered
42. Exclamation of fright
43. Mexican monetary units
45. Eros
47. - de Janeiro
48. Earth
50. Dugong or manatee
52. Smokers receptacle
55. Sand dune
56. Pairs
57. University heads
59. Ostentatious
63. Monetary unit of Romania
64. Planetary model
66. Commercials
67. Tears
68. Monetary unit of Finland
69. Witness
70. S-bends
71. Grass trimming tool

DOWN
1. English county
2. Vow
3. Prefix, ten
4. Hemoglobin deficiency
5. Sexless things
6. Pertaining to the Pharisees
7. Subtle emanation
8. Hit
9. Derived from a halogen
10. Some
11. A peak of the Himalayas
12. Money paid out
13. Gloss
18. Waste drains
22. Comfortably informal
24. Family
26. Name
27. Noose
28. Ireland
29. Greenhouse
30. The east wind
34. Warmness
36. Capital of Western Samoa
37. Inert gaseous element
39. Plunders
41. Most terrible
44. Knight's title
46. Lair
49. Dippers
51. Drew close to
52. Book of maps
53. Type of turnip
54. Lambs
58. Poker stake
60. Encircle
61. Melody
62. Primordial giant in Norse myth
64. Prefix, before
65. Monkey

Puzzle 33

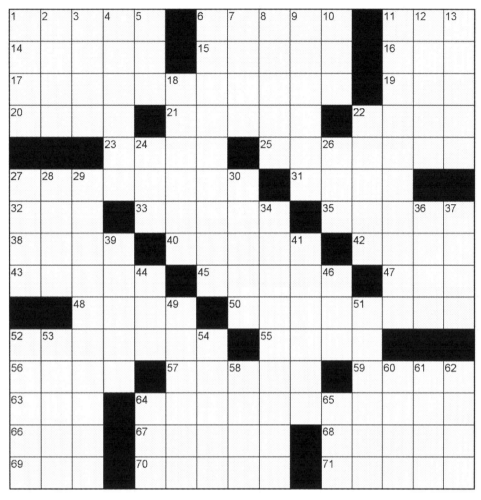

ACROSS
1. Dirt
6. Tantalize
11. Fairy queen
14. Ayers Rock
15. English race course
16. Mature
17. Pertaining to metamorphosis
19. Floor rug
20. Executive Officer
21. Person footing the bill
22. Struck
23. Avid
25. Hard, dense tooth tissue
27. Associates with criminals
31. Nobleman
32. Female sheep
33. Condiment
35. Stories
38. Property title
40. Hurled
42. Father
43. Pertaining to India
45. Serpent
47. Rocky pinnacle
48. Frown
50. Island in central Indonesia
52. Cheese
55. Prince of India
56. Relax
57. Gave birth to (Bible)
59. Prude
63. Ethnic telecaster
64. Italian police
66. Sesame plant
67. Coral island
68. Alcohol burners
69. Pig enclosure
70. Of high moral character
71. Did not

DOWN
1. Vapour
2. Holly
3. Stringed instrument
4. Trails
5. Drone
6. Large spider
7. Glimpse
8. Hurt
9. Evening party
10. Etcetera
11. Having mammillae
12. Once more
13. Actress, - Davis
18. Musical dramas
22. Leash
24. Greek goddess of the dawn
26. Singer, - "King" Cole
27. Basic monetary unit of Ghana
28. Submachine gun
29. Unnecessarily
30. Driving showers
34. Tolerable
36. Epic poetry
37. Hindu garment
39. Electrical rectifier
41. Ice cream made with eggs
44. Rumen
46. British rule in India
49. Wide stiff collar
51. American elk
52. Girdles
53. Acquired pattern of behavior
54. Plunder again
58. Bile
60. Tear apart
61. Republic in SW Asia
62. Romance tale
64. Metal container
65. - Kelly

Puzzle 34

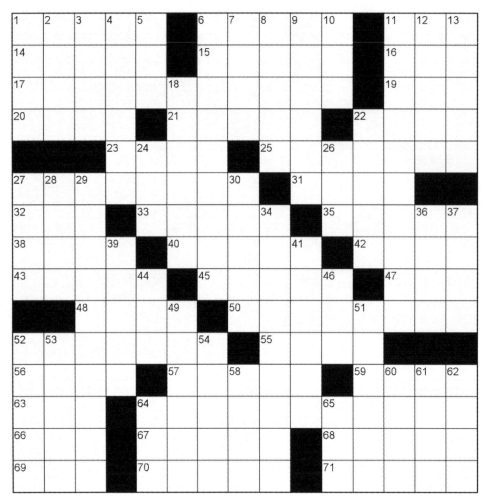

ACROSS
1. Photograph
6. Yellowish resin
11. Food fish
14. Turkish river
15. Dog's lead
16. Fuss
17. Becoming slower
19. Prefix, not
20. Greek god of love
21. Duck with soft down
22. Cozy
23. Officiating priest of a mosque
25. Army engineers
27. Took prisoner
31. Vend
32. Poem
33. Dissuade
35. Claw
38. Rackets
40. Disband troops
42. Stringed toy
43. Rob
45. Majestic
47. Open mesh fabric
48. Arduous journey
50. Pronounce as a nasal sound
52. By the day
55. Tibetan monk
56. Oceans
57. A watch
59. Atop
63. Talent
64. Adrenal gland hormone
66. Falsehood
67. Bundle of sticks
68. Informs
69. My, French (Plural)
70. Long lock of hair
71. Sates

DOWN
1. Funeral fire
2. Perceive sound
3. Capital of Norway
4. Semihard light yellow cheese
5. Bullfight call
6. Flight altitude barometer
7. Honey liquor
8. Curses
9. Apocrypha book
10. 17th letter of the Greek alphabet
11. Tubular pasta
12. Smell
13. Hits or punches (Colloq)
18. Approached
22. Spread
24. Mire
26. Domesticated animal
27. Food fish
28. Entrance
29. Pierces
30. Devil
34. Supporters of the monarchy
36. Town crier's call
37. Short letter
39. Gemstones
41. Igneous rock of a lava flow
44. Garland
46. Thrash
49. Non-stick frying pan lining
51. Bay tree
52. Hymn
53. Strange and mysterious
54. Small biting insect
58. Sticky stuffs
60. Equestrian sport
61. Merely
62. Promontory
64. Toward the stern
65. Etcetera

Puzzle 35

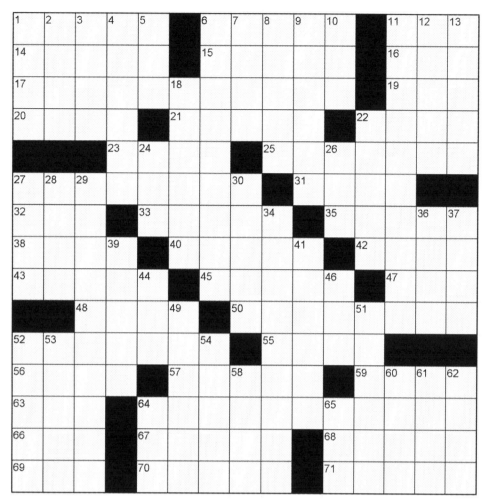

ACROSS
1. Notions
6. Stares
11. Floor covering
14. Consumed again
15. Prefix, wind
16. Reverential fear
17. Stained with blood
19. Automobile
20. Consider
21. Applause
22. Snow runners
23. Indian nursemaid
25. Soft coal
27. Having corners
31. Raccoon
32. Exclamation of surprise
33. Fathers
35. Sum
38. Person in authority
40. Gambler
42. The Pentateuch
43. Broths
45. Something that consumes
47. Attach by stitches
48. Goes to law
50. Turkish sword
52. Ensnares
55. Scene of first miracle
56. Achieve
57. Soother
59. Monetary unit of Iran
63. Kangaroo
64. System of methods
66. Large flightless bird
67. Farewell
68. Nips
69. It is
70. Pools
71. Frighten

DOWN
1. Angered
2. Sandy tract
3. Relaxation
4. Cossack chief
5. Monetary unit of Japan
6. Awkwardness
7. Indigo
8. Of punishment
9. Causing vomiting
10. Turf
11. Rubberized cotton fabric
12. Bide one's time
13. Abrupt
18. Fitted with cogs
22. Snub
24. Yes
26. Obtained
27. Cheats
28. U.S. State
29. Boisterous
30. Rot
34. Having bristles
36. Region
37. Grass around house
39. Scorn
41. Hinder
44. Ocean
46. Hurried
49. Dashboard instrument
51. Pungent bulb plant
52. Heron
53. Mother-in-law of Ruth
54. Glossy
58. Outbuilding
60. Jot
61. Maturing agent
62. Undergo lysis
64. Chart
65. Observation

Puzzle 36

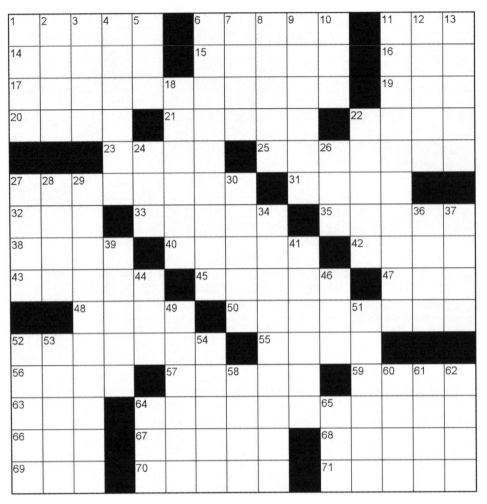

ACROSS
1. Verandah
6. Out of date
11. Food fish
14. Game point
15. Loose fiber used for caulking
16. Fuss
17. Reinforces
19. Prefix, not
20. Carry
21. Took examination again
22. Cozy
23. University head
25. Chats
27. Divides into three
31. Christmas
32. Monetary unit of Japan
33. Percolate
35. Australian cockatoo
38. Appends
40. Lieu
42. Adore
43. Vexes
45. Sign up
47. And not
48. Hood-like membrane
50. Tropical fruit
52. Word formed by transposing letters of another
55. Soft lambskin leather
56. Infants' beds
57. Monetary unit of Zaire
59. Glass bottle
63. Prefix, three
64. Answerable
66. The self
67. Mother-of-pearl
68. Pay for grazing
69. Lair
70. Small drinks of liquor
71. Mexican money

DOWN
1. Surreptitious, attention getting sound
2. Prefix, eight
3. Cheat the system
4. Beliefs
5. Female bird
6. Regent
7. Exclamations of surprise
8. Irish dagger
9. Darkening of the skin by sunlight
10. Printer's measures
11. Tubular pasta
12. Smell
13. Hits or punches (Colloq)
18. Airs and -
22. Rob
24. Conger
26. To clothe
27. Russian emperor
28. Repeat
29. Sign
30. Perfume
34. Diatribes
36. Shakespeare's river
37. Flock of cattle
39. Metal drosses
41. Realm
44. Prefix, over
46. Fold
49. East Indies sailor
51. Lay waste to
52. Played the part of
53. Norwegian name of Norway
54. Moslem holy city
58. Standard
60. Large wading bird
61. Too
62. Permits
64. Besides
65. Faucet

Puzzle 37

ACROSS
1. Soil
6. Test ore for minerals
11. Consumed
14. Swiss mountain
15. Large violin-like instrument
16. Actor, - Chaney
17. Sleight of hand
19. Cover
20. Fine dry soil
21. Oily fruit
22. Bundle
23. Hang droopingly
25. Went in
27. Egg yolk
31. A drink
32. Malt beverage
33. Valleys
35. Brightly coloured lizard
38. Italian currency
40. Sloping walkways
42. Enough
43. Noblemen
45. Angers
47. Beetle
48. Auricular
50. Study of sexual behavior
52. Neck artery
55. Egypt's river
56. Certainly
57. Necessities
59. Stupid person
63. Vapour
64. Unfortunate
66. Part of verb to be
67. Full speed
68. Useful
69. Colour
70. Contraction of has not
71. Flower part

DOWN
1. Castrate
2. Stead
3. Ova
4. Cockroach
5. Go wrong
6. Being without cells
7. Prefix, part
8. Bondsman
9. Foreigners
10. Over there
11. Becoming slower and broader
12. Fine linen
13. Finished
18. Monetary unit
22. Light grayish brown
24. Advanced in years
26. Two
27. Valley
28. Hip bones
29. Tyrannised
30. Lead ups to finals
34. Lustrous
36. Music synthesiser
37. Askew
39. Singers
41. Involving sexism
44. Be seated
46. The sun
49. Picture theater
51. Envoy
52. Cheroot
53. Conscious
54. Remove harmful vapours from
58. Ireland
60. Funeral notice
61. Earthen pot
62. Sense
64. Cheer
65. Sheep

Puzzle 38

ACROSS
1. Frequented by rooks
6. Put
11. Poke
14. Give consent
15. Pass on
16. To endure
17. To compel
19. Piece
20. Freshwater duck
21. Show emotion
22. Cipher
23. Jaguarundi
25. Worker ants
27. Open air
31. Worn by women in India
32. Crooked
33. Construct
35. Coffee
38. East Indies palm
40. Cease being awake
42. South-east Asian nation
43. Vista
45. Agreements
47. Fly larva
48. Prophet
50. Japanese dish
52. Cork
55. Motion picture
56. Situate
57. Egyptian capital
59. Foot cover
63. Illustrative craft
64. Lowering in dignity
66. Shelter
67. Own to
68. Second largest violin
69. Sea (French)
70. Contract
71. Rendezvous

DOWN
1. Rave
2. Double curve
3. Killer whale
4. Having stabiliser fin
5. Affirmative reply
6. Chiefly
7. Mother of Apollo
8. Winged
9. Purveys
10. Organ of sight
11. Brazilian evergreen tree
12. Tolerate
13. Units of computer memory
18. Resembling serum
22. Song
24. Teenage lout
26. Leg
27. 3 Admits
28. Of urine
29. Compositor
30. Rain and snow
34. To profane
36. Crook
37. Italian wine province
39. Anoint
41. Portion of time
44. Snakelike fish
46. Transgression
49. Ebb
51. Prefix, time before
52. Sacred song
53. Person hiring
54. Molten material
58. Greek goddess of the rainbow
60. Greasy
61. Mountain passes
62. Nautical mile
64. Indian dish
65. Statute

Puzzle 39

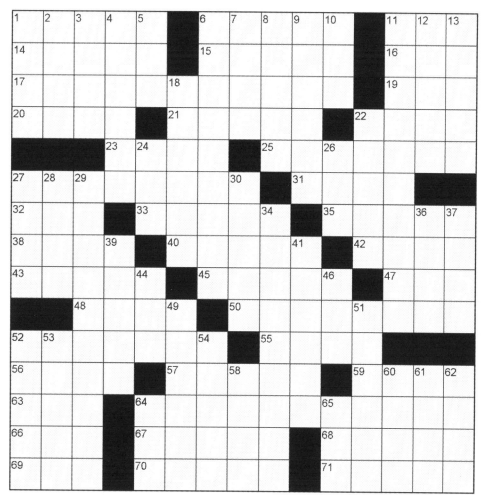

ACROSS
1. Clergyman
6. Sorceress
11. Explosive sound
14. Satire
15. Worship
16. Atomic mass unit
17. Dramatic
19. Corded fabric
20. At sea
21. Very small island
22. The three wise men
23. Camp shelter
25. Of ten
27. Medicinal plant
31. Ruined city in W Iran
32. Honey insect
33. Monetary unit of Sierra Leone
35. Tam
38. Prohibits
40. Precipitates
42. Split apart
43. Mountain ridge
45. Roman garments
47. Garbage can
48. Rough earthenware
50. Nine times as much
52. Adage
55. Pleasing
56. Be defeated
57. Procreate
59. Hindu music
63. Prefix, one
64. Amber-colored candy
66. Encountered
67. Interior
68. Hipbone
69. Oriental sauce
70. Numbers 13 through 19
71. Hangs

DOWN
1. Entry permit
2. Angers
3. Ice-cream holder
4. Having a handle
5. Handwoven Scandinavian rug
6. Vest
7. Object of worship
8. Coloured
9. Wooden boxes
10. Norse goddess
11. Capital of Suriname
12. Greek letter
13. Student
18. Smaller
22. Tight-fisted person
24. Former measure of length
26. Young bear
27. Title of respect for God
28. Close
29. Munificence
30. Negatively charged ion
34. Machinery experts
36. Sinister
37. Nurse
39. Staff (Music)
41. Sense
44. Supplement existence
46. Not sweet
49. Sophisticated
51. Cane used for punishment
52. Stone fruit
53. Copy with stencils
54. Swiss capital
58. Valley
60. Against
61. Showy ornament
62. 3 Weapons
64. Mouthpiece of a bridle
65. Small drink

Puzzle 40

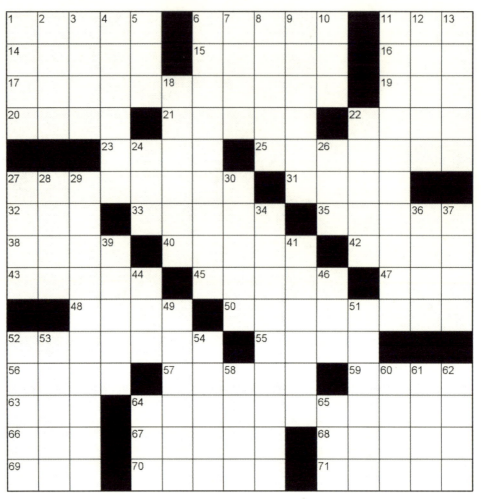

ACROSS
1. Measured out
6. Suit
11. Color
14. Playing marble
15. Grassy plain
16. Evening
17. Exclusive attention to material prosperity
19. New Guinea seaport
20. 6th month of the Jewish calendar
21. View
22. Floating vegetable matter
23. Police informer
25. Stupors
27. First name
31. This thing
32. Supplement
33. Educate
35. Abreast
38. Takes a seat
40. Fragrant flower
42. Scorning person
43. Goat antelope
45. Tag
47. Male swan
48. Exclamations of surprise
50. Unwearying
52. Encode
55. Polynesian carved image
56. Fly larvae
57. Duty rosters
59. At the apex
63. Japanese sash
64. Imaginary
66. Entirely
67. Monetary unit of Saudi Arabia
68. Chemical compound
69. Golf peg
70. Sleeping noise
71. First prime minister of India

DOWN
1. Mother
2. Mild oath
3. Good-bye (2-2)
4. Eternal (Poet)
5. The (German)
6. Extortion by intimidation
7. Australian super-model
8. Lacking brightness
9. Put in
10. Male cat
11. Unwillingness
12. Avoid
13. Acts
18. Republic in SW Asia
22. Breaks suddenly
24. Insect
26. Exclamation of surprise
27. Heraldry, wide horizontal stripe on shield
28. Migrant farm worker
29. Capable of being drawn back
30. Showy actions
34. Livable
36. Dove's calls
37. Wanes
39. Flies high
41. Moderate to deep red
44. For what reason
46. Monetary unit of Albania
49. Rick
51. Maintain contact
52. Torpedo vessel (1-4)
53. Aristocratic
54. Japan's Capital
58. Rip
60. 9th letter of the Hebrew alphabet
61. Finished
62. Republic in W South America
64. Missus
65. Pet form of Leonard

Puzzle 41

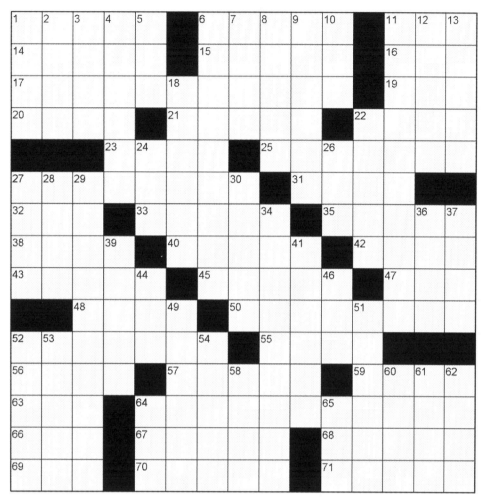

ACROSS
1. Tar
6. International code
11. Exploit
14. Habituate
15. At right angles to a ships length
16. Arrest
17. Fortresses
19. Invest with nickname
20. Beancurd
21. Breathed rattlingly
22. Allot
23. Emperor of Russia
25. Narrowed
27. Strongly expressive
31. Fail to hit
32. Metal rod
33. Mexican money
35. Unclothed
38. Ink stain
40. Arab vessels
42. Location
43. Cuttlefish pigment
45. Intestinal obstruction
47. Regret
48. Heroic
50. In a series
52. Guilty person
55. Division of a school year
56. Inwardly
57. Naked pictures
59. Blessing
63. By way of
64. Spitefully
66. Long period of time
67. Leg joint
68. Stage whisper
69. An explosive
70. Renee -, Australian rock singer
71. Spook

DOWN
1. Nuisance
2. Towards the centre
3. Lawn
4. Cringe
5. Female bird
6. Hindu religious sage
7. Ancient Greek coin
8. Rent out again
9. - Hussein
10. Printer's measures
11. Petticoat
12. Fry lightly
13. Grew less
18. Rasped
22. Rocky tablelands
24. Move quickly
26. Transfix
27. Recedes
28. Man
29. Propelling agent
30. Chills
34. Sugar
36. Sewing case
37. Hold as an opinion
39. Liable to tip over
41. Most certain
44. Atmosphere
46. Title of a knight
49. Cineol derivative
51. Waylay
52. Musk-yielding cat
53. Federation
54. Having long, protruding teeth
58. Delete (Printing)
60. Potpourri
61. One's parents (Colloq)
62. Russian no
64. Tatter
65. Tire

Puzzle 42

ACROSS
1. Tenor
6. Abrade
11. Once existed
14. Church walkway
15. Showed film again
16. Colour
17. Nobodies
19. Anger
20. Suffix, diminutive
21. An anaesthetic
22. Celestial body
23. Rattan
25. Female lion
27. Rulers
31. Female sheep
32. New Zealand bird
33. Weaves wool
35. Tibetan monks
38. Lazily
40. More painful
42. Chest
43. Reset sights
45. Backs of necks
47. Golfers mound
48. Side
50. Turkish saber
52. Pertaining to an axilla
55. Uncivil
56. Repair
57. Earthwork
59. Skirt coming to just below knee
63. An age
64. Expunges
66. Piece
67. Loud noise
68. African antelope
69. Top card
70. Determined gender of
71. Throws

DOWN
1. Norseman
2. Public disturbance
3. Is not
4. Wool
5. Cardinal number
6. Standard of judgment
7. 8th letter of the Hebrew alphabet
8. Shakespearian sprite
9. Fairyland
10. Abstract being
11. Tinsmith
12. Subtle emanations
13. Prophets
18. Wood joints
22. Slink
24. Noah's vessel
26. Nocturnal bird
27. Islamic chieftain
28. Style
29. Territory under a palatine
30. Wander
34. Parted
36. Seaward
37. Type of gun
39. Cede
41. Readjust pitch of musical instrument
44. - de mer, seasickness
46. Morose
49. Taw
51. Part of the Talmud
52. One-celled protozoa
53. Adapted to a dry environment
54. Ease
58. Dreadful
60. Inflammation (Suffix)
61. Something owing
62. Egyptian goddess of fertility
64. Observation
65. Fabulous bird

Puzzle 43

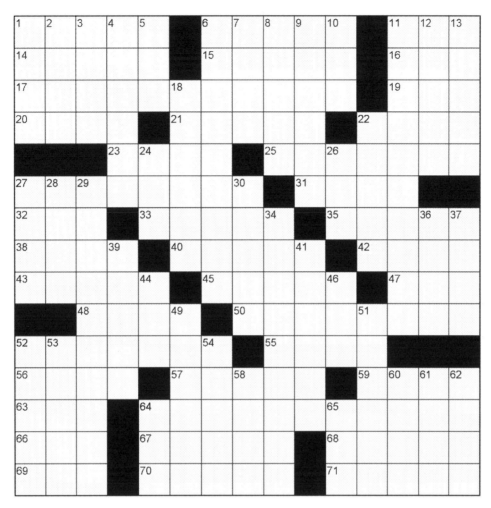

ACROSS
1. Cape
6. Take as one's own
11. Choice marble
14. Alert
15. Television
16. Period of history
17. Merry festivity
19. Outfit
20. Italian city
21. Lower portion of the small intestine
22. American Indian
23. U.S. space agency
25. Distilling vessel
27. Pagans
31. Naive person
32. Observation
33. Bowed
35. Shrouds
38. Proboscis
40. Cry out loudly
42. Drop moisture
43. Tolling of bells at death
45. The east wind
47. Impair
48. States
50. Pertaining to the cutting and polishing of stones
52. In place of
55. Lake
56. American coin
57. Pertaining to ships of war
59. Questions
63. Period of human life
64. Appointment to higher house
66. Female fowl
67. Agave fibre
68. Garlic-flavored mayonnaise
69. Food scrap
70. Direct
71. Abdomen of a crustacean

DOWN
1. Temporary settlement
2. Monetary unit of Angola
3. Paddles
4. Unmitigated
5. Lock opener
6. Large mass of sliding snow
7. Levee
8. Hatred
9. Copyist
10. To clothe
11. Dry land
12. Zodiac sign
13. Pay
18. Tight-fisted people
22. Bawled
24. Exclamation of surprise
26. 23rd letter of the Hebrew alphabet
27. Goose cry
28. Black
29. Appraisal
30. South Korea's capital
34. Fibrous membrane of the brain
36. Fibber
37. Agile
39. Overjoy
41. Black gum
44. Soap ingredient
46. Knight's title
49. Wisest
51. Clockwise
52. State in the NW United States
53. African river
54. "Inferno" author
58. Dell
60. Foot covering
61. Thousand
62. Reel
64. Sister
65. Knock vigorously

Puzzle 44

ACROSS
1. Nidi
6. Standard of perfection
11. Slender metal fastener
14. Greetings
15. Rob
16. Single unit
17. Translated clearly
19. Prompt
20. Once again
21. Oilcan
22. Slide
23. Redact
25. Lesser roads
27. Blind alley
31. Coal dust
32. Small truck
33. Suffix, diminutives
35. Pertaining to a tube
38. Book leaf
40. Watery animal fluid
42. Ear part
43. The Hindu Destroyer
45. Warehouse
47. Observation
48. Savoury Mexican dish
50. Toothed wheel
52. Arachnids
55. Ore deposit
56. Large volume
57. Unadorned
59. Uncouth
63. America (Abbr)
64. Hereditary anemia
66. Ballpoint biro
67. Dray
68. Founder of the Mogul Empire
69. Pigpen
70. Beginning
71. Narrow openings

DOWN
1. Soft lambskin leather
2. Dash
3. Annoyed
4. Melted
5. Plant juice
6. Vexed
7. Distribute cards
8. Relaxes
9. Wards off
10. Captained
11. Handbag
12. Eskimo
13. Of necessity
18. Raises (Flag)
22. Capital of South Korea
24. Scottish river
26. Decay
27. Drinking vessels
28. American state
29. Being legitimate
30. Roman goddess of agriculture
34. Petitioner
36. French clergyman
37. For fear that
39. Elude
41. Idiots
44. Very skilled person
46. Fox
49. Parentless child
51. Grain
52. Butts
53. Postulate
54. Metal drosses
58. Agave
60. Boss on a shield
61. Daily fare of food
62. Hearing organs
64. A couple
65. Ethnic telecaster

Puzzle 45

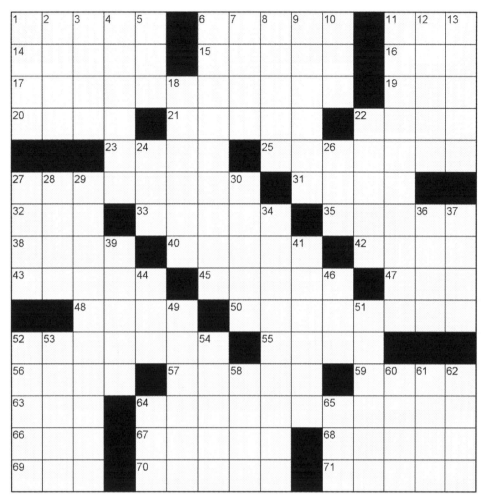

ACROSS
1. Angry
6. Small islands
11. Taxicab
14. Tidal wave
15. Scrounge
16. Atomic mass unit
17. Person who likes cats
19. Not (prefix)
20. Leg joint
21. Bed quilt
22. Cosy
23. Dirt
25. Non-sleeping compartments
27. Resembling an elytron
31. Monetary unit of Cambodia
32. Alas
33. More attractive in a strange way
35. Prison rooms
38. Former
40. Tendon
42. Eurasian crow
43. Relabel
45. Urban
47. No
48. Periods of history
50. Curative potion
52. Lengthen
55. Advise
56. Negative votes
57. Finds shelter
59. View
63. Primate
64. The study of aging
66. New Zealand parrot
67. Rephrase
68. Dried coconut kernel
69. Sin
70. Burdens
71. Thing of value

DOWN
1. Feeble
2. Precipitation
3. Leer
4. Most accurate
5. Pronoun
6. Not politic
7. London district
8. Hips
9. Chocolate and cream delicacy
10. That woman
11. Tubular pasta
12. Love affair
13. Stoppers
18. Hateful
22. Guide
24. Killer whale
26. Facial twitch
27. Pitcher
28. Tradition
29. During the recent past
30. Jeans fabric
34. Ministers
36. Advance money
37. Inner Hebrides island
39. Vetches
41. Broadest
44. Gun (Slang)
46. Spanish hero
49. Diagram
51. Large violin-like instruments
52. Serpent
53. Become narrow
54. Rented
58. Finished
60. Expression used when accident happens
61. Monster
62. Monetary unit of Burma
64. Girl or woman
65. Wood sorrel

Puzzle 46

ACROSS
1. Pule
6. Seal of a papal bull
11. Plant juice
14. Brother of Moses
15. Assumed name
16. Black bird
17. Thinness
19. Negative
20. Rubber pipe
21. Peruses
22. Male deer
23. British National Gallery
25. Member of a sect
27. Spell incorrectly
31. Appear
32. Carp-like fish
33. Scandinavian mythical demon
35. Sandy bathing beach
38. Cheats
40. Garden pest
42. Extent of space
43. Winged
45. Scope
47. - and outs, intricacies
48. Expression
50. One of Jason's crew
52. Makeshift
55. River in central Switzerland
56. Paddles
57. Performances by two
59. Title of respect for God
63. Japanese sash
64. Reef of coral
66. Hawaiian acacia
67. Spanish, friend
68. Tropical plant used in cosmetics
69. The sun
70. Devil
71. More unusual

DOWN
1. Cleanse
2. Nimbus
3. Angers
4. Compositions for nine
5. Finish
6. Seaport in NE Spain
7. Arm bone
8. Charges over property
9. Girls
10. Donkey
11. Flagship of Columbus
12. Anigh
13. Young pig
18. Chemical compounds
22. Gravestone
24. Fitting
26. Brown-capped boletus mushroom
27. Flaky mineral
28. Image of a deity
29. Consisting of senators
30. South American beast
34. Oscillatory motion
36. Knee
37. The Orient
39. Paces
41. Synthetase
44. Work unit
46. Rocky pinnacle
49. Title for a woman
51. Approached
52. Cry-babies
53. Forbidden
54. Jewish festival
58. Therefore
60. Curve
61. Prefix, well
62. Distant
64. Not good
65. 17th letter of the Greek alphabet

Puzzle 47

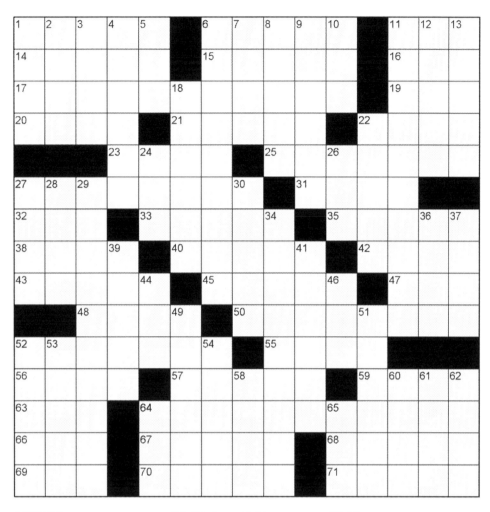

ACROSS
1. Aviates
6. Epileptic seizure
11. 9th letter of the Hebrew alphabet
14. Sum up
15. Backbone
16. Cereal grass
17. Perform better than expected
19. Wrath
20. Pith
21. Cave
22. Norse god
23. Robust
25. Resembling silver
27. Pulse
31. Mortgage
32. Affirmative reply
33. Cartoon character, - Fudd
35. Go in
38. Mould
40. Warble
42. Hindu garment
43. Anesthetic
45. African antelope
47. Apex
48. Impudent child
50. Pleasantness
52. Root vegetable
55. Silent
56. Drug-yielding plant
57. 3rd letter of the Hebrew alphabet
59. Sealed with a kiss
63. Today
64. A rough draft
66. Information
67. Upright
68. Italian lady
69. Donkey
70. S-bends
71. Command

DOWN
1. Amphibian
2. Son of Jacob and Leah
3. Frozen confections
4. Sensual
5. Mineral spring
6. Long-tailed mongoose
7. Voucher
8. Rows
9. Reveal to view
10. Witness
11. Having three teeth
12. Monetary unit of Iceland
13. Tiny
18. Serenely
22. Kilns
24. Mature
26. Falsehood
27. Stable attendant
28. Bog fuel
29. Potato dish
30. Portable chair
34. Military groups
36. Greek god of love
37. Tears
39. Curt
41. Small compartment or chamber
44. Fled
46. Soak flax
49. Striped cats
51. Wise old man
52. Machete
53. Agaves
54. Heaps
58. Small rodents
60. Stream of air
61. First-class
62. Knot in wood
64. Scottish river
65. Fuss

Puzzle 48

ACROSS
1. Invalidate
6. Desert plants
11. Sphere
14. Consumed again
15. Bestow
16. Female ruff
17. Asexual reproduction
19. Cheat
20. Crack
21. South American mountains
22. Leg part
23. To the inside of
25. Noble
27. Longtime resident of Hawaii
31. Female sheep
32. Before
33. Purgative injection
35. Leave undisturbed (3.2)
38. Lets head fall wearily
40. Rock cavity
42. School dance
43. Identical people
45. Watery
47. Limb
48. Dove's calls
50. Act out a particular event (4-4)
52. Affected by scabs
55. Supernatural force
56. Overacts
57. The gripes
59. Cormorant
63. Frozen water
64. A rough draft
66. Human race
67. Dropsy
68. Reddish brown dye
69. Drunkard
70. Engage in wedeln
71. Serpent

DOWN
1. 3 Weapons
2. Inert gaseous element
3. Grandmother
4. Ideal land
5. Limb
6. Artilleryman
7. Overwhelmed
8. Instances
9. Sad
10. Egos
11. Resembling an orchestra
12. Lubricate again
13. Amphetamine tablet
18. Consuming
22. Precipitous
24. Not
26. Shoemaker's tool
27. English county
28. In a line
29. Remedy
30. Love affair
34. Word that modifies a noun
36. Aboriginal rite
37. U.S. TV award
39. Scorning persons
41. Entwine
44. Weep
46. Monetary unit of Japan
49. Formally withdraw from
51. Glued
52. Spacing wedges
53. Source of cocoa
54. Apportioned
58. Citrus fruit
60. Posterior
61. First-class
62. Growl
64. Nocturnal precipitation
65. Exclamation of surprise

Puzzle 49

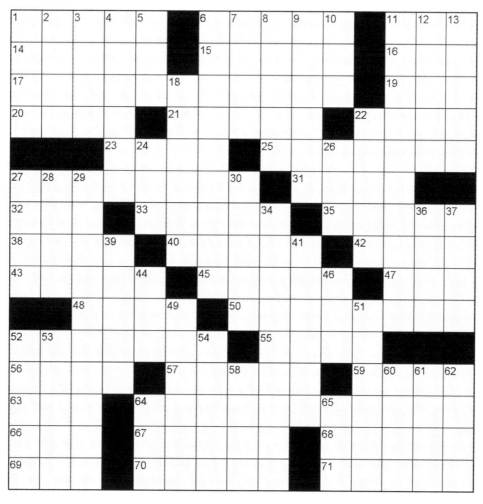

ACROSS
1. Circular plates
6. Seraglio
11. Beverage made with beaten eggs
14. Habituate
15. Evergreen tree
16. Japanese sash
17. Hand tool
19. Extinct flightless bird
20. Natter
21. Flower
22. Capital of Yemen
23. Peak
25. Most musty
27. Intoxicating liquor
31. Slide
32. Hawaiian acacia
33. Confused hand-to-hand fight
35. Faded
38. Entrance
40. Infant's loincloth
42. Fijian capital
43. Polynesian edible roots
45. Lout
47. Actor, - Gibson
48. Oceans
50. Legal jargon
52. Llamas
55. Bog
56. Vehicles
57. City in W Germany
59. Ambition
63. Israeli submachine gun
64. Ironically
66. Convert into leather
67. Small antelope
68. Collection of maps
69. Work unit
70. Diminished
71. Torment

DOWN
1. Circular plate
2. Small measure
3. Chapter of the Koran
4. Native of Crete
5. Stitch
6. Boisterous play
7. Got down from mount
8. Splits
9. Turns inside out
10. Sea (French)
11. Pen name (3.2.5)
12. Hautboys
13. Huge
18. Make moist
22. Assumed name
24. Eccentric shaft
26. Peak
27. Card game
28. Musical ending
29. Spring used for timepiece
30. Flower part
34. Mayfly
36. Days before
37. Broad valley
39. New Guinea currency units
41. Woman who practices yoga
44. Cyst envelope
46. Paddle
49. Desert in N Africa
51. Emissary
52. Sharp
53. Leper
54. Glossy fabric
58. Deride
60. Earthen pot
61. Exclamation to express sorrow
62. Undergo lysis
64. Female pig
65. Small domesticated carnivore

Puzzle 50

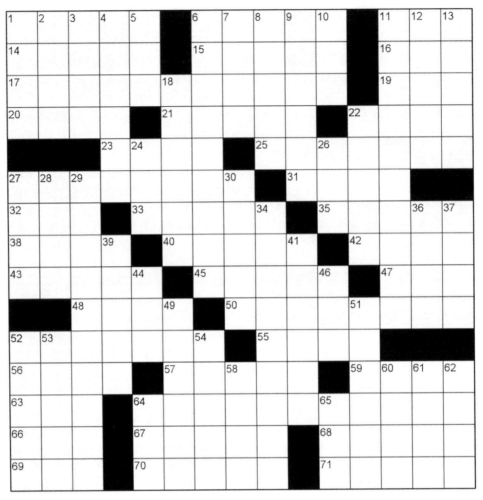

ACROSS
1. Heavens
6. Cabdriver
11. Monkey
14. Venomous snake
15. Conscious
16. - Kelly
17. Spontaneous generation
19. Two-year old sheep
20. The majority
21. Took examination again
22. Talk irrationally
23. Angers
25. Let down
27. Demon in female form
31. Narcotics agent
32. Fire remains
33. Brass wind instrument
35. Courageous
38. Lake or pond
40. Sweatbox
42. East Indies palm
43. Light refractor
45. Theatrical parody
47. Minced oath
48. Jump
50. Degenerate
52. Ex-serviceman
55. Bome to be without
56. Affirm with confidence
57. Revolving part
59. Throws softly
63. Rummy game
64. Not reparable
66. Malt beverage
67. Ditch
68. Utterly stupid person
69. Hallucinogenic drug
70. Cancels a deletion
71. Vesta

DOWN
1. Swindle
2. Monetary unit of Nigeria
3. Sacred Egyptian bird
4. Arousing sexual desire
5. Droop
6. Sugar obtained from sugarcane
7. Inspires dread
8. Of a base
9. Native of Britain
10. Affirmative response
11. Most southerly continent
12. Annoy
13. Bordered
18. Antarctic volcano
22. Television repeat
24. Chafe
26. Humorous person
27. Coarsely ground corn
28. A person that uses
29. Named
30. Veered
34. Covers for letters
36. Dot
37. Lively
39. Gravel ridge
41. Dawn goddess
44. Russian community
46. Greek goddess of the dawn
49. Cockatoo or galah
51. Ethiopian baboon
52. Pertaining to a vagus nerve
53. Sins
54. Scandinavian
58. Trial
60. Funeral notice
61. Cartel
62. Third son of Adam
64. Possibilities
65. Edge

Puzzle 51

ACROSS
1. Closes hard
6. Based on eight
11. Automobile
14. Outrigger
15. Carried
16. Japanese sash
17. Surprising
19. Very modern
20. A legume
21. Shoulder scarf of fur
22. Complacent
23. Australian explorer
25. To produce milk
27. Sword-shaped
31. Something lent
32. Nae
33. Daring
35. One -, prejudiced
38. 3 Weapons
40. Charges over property
42. Prefix, ten
43. Re-choose
45. Mediterranean island
47. Go wrong
48. Lath
50. Preliminary test
52. Existing power
structure
55. Paste
56. Monetary unit of Thailand
57. Custom
59. Metal spike
63. Dined
64. Mutability
66. An evergreen
67. Anoint
68. Wearies
69. Pedal digit
70. Located
71. Confidence tricks

DOWN
1. Strike breaker
2. Cut with laser
3. Rectangular pier
4. Behaved listlessly
5. Monetary unit of Japan
6. Pertaining to childbirth
7. Small salmon
8. Warble
9. Fuse pottery or glass
10. Lower limb
11. Seize arbitrarily
12. Around
13. Crest
18. Republic in SW Asia
22. Sober
24. - and Yang
26. Long-leaved lettuce
27. Growl
28. Traditional knowledge
29. Air
30. Turn inside out
34. Gave power to
36. Colour of unbleached linen
37. Mend socks
39. Wet slapping sound
41. Marsh birds
44. Sailor
46. French, water
49. Food paste
51. Living in still water
52. Behind
53. Courtyard
54. Be silent
58. Liquid secreted by the liver
60. Distinctive quality
61. As previously given
62. Minus
64. Vessel or duct
65. It is

Puzzle 52

ACROSS
1. Fathered
6. Greek cheese
11. Magazine
14. Prefix, wind
15. Mistake
16. Australian bird
17. Astound
19. Obtained
20. Jaguarundi
21. Weaving machines
22. Separate
23. Secular
25. Punishment
27. Random mating
31. Worn by women in India
32. Monetary unit of Romania
33. Electrical rectifier
35. Toss
38. Vases
40. Regretting
42. Begone
43. Variety of coffee
45. Gannet
47. Revised form of Esperanto
48. Jot
50. Hushed
52. Non-professional
55. Ballot
56. Fragments
57. Monarch
59. As well as
63. French, water
64. Tyrannising
66. Rocky peak
67. Greek goddess of peace
68. Theatrical entertainment
69. Take to court
70. Having long neck hairs
71. Waterbird

DOWN
1. Secure
2. Inwardly
3. The back of
4. Preserve corpse
5. Tell on
6. Savage
7. Therefore
8. Trudge
9. Throws
10. Illustrative craft
11. Large
12. Lifeless
13. Tough
18. Tonic
22. French capital
24. Assist
26. Doze
27. A stone fruit
28. Air (prefix)
29. Office of a nuncio
30. Farewell
34. Invigorated
36. Message symbols
37. Head covering
39. Rounds of ammunition
41. In abundance
44. Consumed
46. Seine
49. Roman goddess of the dawn
51. Closer
52. Wrongfully assists
53. Mew
54. Cud
58. Queue
60. Survive
61. Ignore
62. Double curve
64. Hazy
65. Unit of energy

Puzzle 53

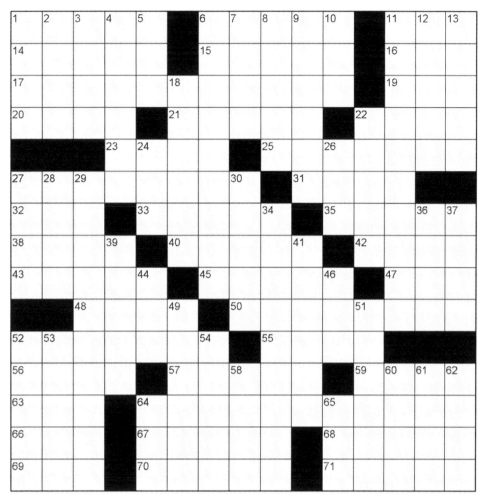

ACROSS
1. Wharves
6. In bad health (Colloq)
11. Electrical unit
14. Belief involving sorcery
15. Vapid
16. New Guinea seaport
17. Mutual relation
19. Actor, - Chaney
20. Derived from a ketone
21. Stop prematurely
22. Fronded plant
23. Identical
25. Earache
27. Person who makes firearms
31. Of you
32. Land measure
33. Conjunction
35. Yacht stabilisers
38. Tires
40. Land measures
42. Portico
43. Failures
45. Wiser
47. Metallic element
48. Rip
50. Listening device common with portable music systems
52. Laments
55. Domesticate
56. Make healthy
57. Denude
59. Not kosher
63. Long-sleeved linen vestment
64. Forever hereafter
66. Naught
67. Avoid
68. Stories
69. Top card
70. The populous
71. Poker stakes

DOWN
1. Wharf
2. Musical instrument
3. Certainty (Colloq)
4. Rug of animal skins
5. Fem. pronoun
6. Persons suffering from disease causing blood-sugar abnormalities
7. To the inside of
8. Capital of Egypt
9. Tangled
10. Japanese currency
11. Graceful
12. New Zealand aboriginal
13. Contour feather
18. Thin plate
22. Chimney pipes
24. Atomic mass unit
26. Very good (1-2)
27. Fishing hook
28. Mountain range
29. Capable of being negotiated
30. Greek goddesses of the seasons
34. Reverse image photos
36. Meat cut
37. Sensible
39. Ascend
41. Shawl worn in Mexico
44. Saveloy
46. Rotational speed
49. Put a new sole on
51. Cossack chief
52. Republic in W Africa
53. Memento
54. Twang guitar strings
58. Repeat
60. Cheat the system
61. Sea eagle
62. Heraldry, wide horizontal stripe on shield
64. Gave food to
65. Handwoven Scandinavian rug

Puzzle 54

ACROSS
1. Cubed
6. Urge forward
11. Involuntary muscular contraction
14. Isolated
15. Agree total
16. Exclamation of wonder
17. Group of firefighters
19. Prefix, one
20. Abound
21. Join
22. Proper
23. Showing unusual talent
25. Concentrated extract
27. Large-eyed, Indonesian monkeys
31. The Pentateuch
32. Mature
33. Vestige
35. Musical beat
38. Car registration (Colloq)
40. Scorning persons
42. Prophet
43. First
45. Feel
47. Negative
48. Sorghum
50. Flexibly
52. Premature
55. Veinlike deposit
56. Vandals
57. Ship room
59. Increases
63. Fitting
64. Earthly
66. Large body of water
67. Canvas-like fabric
68. Manila hemp plant
69. Conger
70. Scottish, concerning
71. Compound tissue in vascular plants

DOWN
1. Foolish
2. Tennis star, - Natase
3. Heart
4. Purgative injections
5. Debutante
6. Traveling from place to place
7. The wise men
8. Item of crockery
9. Oldest
10. Alkali
11. Contest
12. Grecian architectural style
13. Hourly clock sound
18. Monarchs
22. Fathers
24. Mouthpiece of a bridle
26. Drunkard
27. Tarpaulin
28. Maturing agent
29. Pertaining to a regiment
30. Ladle
34. Bubbling with excitement
36. Skin
37. Wild revelry
39. Excludes
41. Descendants
44. Bullfight call
46. Possessed
49. Red dye
51. Close at hand
52. Stage
53. Monetary unit of India
54. Margarine
58. Ground husk of wheat
60. Face
61. Fresh-water fish
62. Close hard
64. Two
65. Duty

Puzzle 55

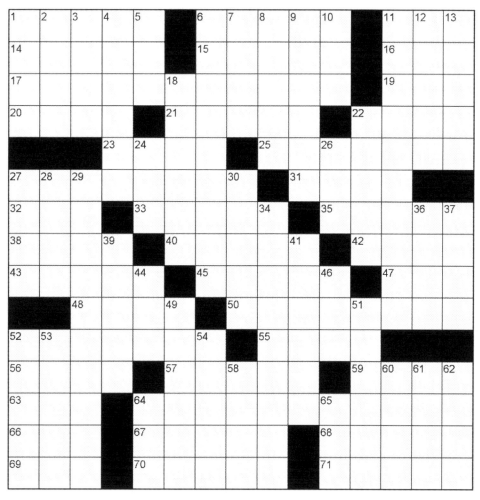

ACROSS
1. Blowing in gusts
6. Principle
11. Twosome
14. Unbind
15. Erse
16. Sin
17. Doubtfully
19. By way of
20. - sapiens, Man
21. Fine fur
22. Marine mammal
23. Froth
25. Ambles
27. Historic county in S Scotland
31. Performance by one
32. Small truck
33. Fortune-telling cards
35. Roman god of carnal love
38. Freshwater fish
40. Pulls
42. Team
43. Pierce
45. Napery
47. At the present time
48. Performs
50. Bravely
52. State of being acid
55. Motion picture
56. Cattle lows
57. Rebind
59. Word used in comparisons
63. French, good
64. Crust of the earth
66. Meadow
67. Farewell
68. Weird
69. Snakelike fish
70. Agreements
71. Great fear

DOWN
1. Spurt forth
2. Remarkable
3. Stalk
4. Warning
5. To date
6. Having two branches
7. Semite
8. Window ledges
9. Small isles
10. Bashful
11. Growing
12. Wild sheep of S Asia
13. Verbal exams
18. Book of the Bible
22. Alone
24. Food scrap
26. Fabled bird
27. Air channel
28. State in the W United States
29. Resembling a meridian
30. Not hollow
34. Stubborn, obstinate
36. Image of a deity
37. Moist with dew
39. Jabs
41. Progression
44. Wreath of flowers
46. A fool
49. Take long steps
51. Lower
52. Stroll
53. Bush call
54. Abominable snowmen
58. You
60. In this place
61. Melody
62. Requirement
64. Put Down
65. Prefix, foot

Puzzle 56

ACROSS
1. North Vietnam's capital
6. Garrets
11. Sister
14. Fuming sulphuric acid
15. Fourth month
16. An explosive
17. Lucidity
19. Regret
20. Gael
21. Assail
22. Undoing
23. Looker
25. Imperfections
27. Nonsense
31. Engrossed
32. Part of verb to be
33. Saltpeter
35. Uncertainty
38. Illegally fixes result
40. Sponsorship
42. Threesome
43. Intense hatred
45. Judicial rulings
47. High mountain
48. Raced
50. Aztec temple
52. Of the spleen
55. Verse
56. Scorch
57. Of the nose
59. Strong woody fiber
63. Breakfast cereal
64. Summarize
66. Avail of
67. Actress, - Davis
68. Wading bird
69. Colour
70. Prickly plant
71. Worries

DOWN
1. Brewing ingredients
2. Smart - , show-off
3. Emperor of Rome 54-68
4. Evicted
5. Little devil
6. Torn
7. Musical work
8. Cooked in oil
9. Giggle
10. Wily
11. Morphological
12. Eskimo
13. Submachine guns
18. Spain and Portugal
22. Transplant plant
24. Monetary unit of Japan
26. A craze
27. Gambling game
28. Parched
29. Made law
30. Lawful
34. Chinese paper
36. Duck's beak
37. Pith helmet
39. Great
41. Backless seats
44. Adult males
46. Very skilled person
49. A meal
51. Stroller
52. Scrub
53. Facet
54. Desert plants
58. Cloy
60. River in central Switzerland
61. Springing gait
62. Decades
64. Wane
65. Television frequency

Puzzle 57

ACROSS
1. Portents
6. Test ore for minerals
11. Cyst envelope
14. Recipient
15. Useful
16. A couple
17. Fragments
19. Knock with knuckles
20. Pause
21. Something that consumes
22. Compel
23. Secular
25. Broadened
27. Aversion
31. A fool
32. Garland
33. Fulcrum for an oar
35. Dutch flower
38. Small dog
40. Debonair
42. Grain store
43. Submachine guns
45. Quickly
47. A fool
48. Lowest high tide
50. Whipped severely
52. Tremulous effect
55. Hour
56. Simple
57. Pertaining to the ear
59. Specific thing indicated
63. Commercials
64. Refusing to obey
66. Falsehood
67. Based on eight
68. Join
69. Distress signal
70. Intervening
71. Nobleman

DOWN
1. Scent
2. Style
3. Finishes
4. Snuggle
5. Ocean
6. Fearless
7. Printer's mark, keep
8. Tendon
9. Second man on the moon
10. Affirmative reply
11. Throttling
12. Rouse
13. Managed
18. Equine sounds
22. Lists of dishes
24. Talent
26. Speck
27. Peaks
28. English court
29. Images
30. Talons
34. Able to be ousted
36. Tennis star, - Natase
37. Pool
39. Foe
41. Star (Heraldry)
44. Cracker biscuit
46. Drone
49. European flatfish
51. Eye part
52. Freshwater ducks
53. Electromagnetic telecommunication
54. Evicts
58. Brown and white horse
60. Scion
61. Towards the centre
62. Submachine gun
64. Benedictine monk's title
65. Name

Puzzle 58

ACROSS
1. Cannabis
6. Child's building cube
11. Fruit conserve
14. Strange and mysterious
15. Bounder
16. Reverential fear
17. Mains power
19. Ingot
20. Antiaircraft fire
21. Living
22. Eroded
23. Wicked
25. Manorial lands
27. Congregation
31. Maori image
32. Exclamation of surprise
33. Instruct
35. Cults
38. Vex
40. Nose
42. Hindu garment
43. Climb
45. Walk
47. Wager
48. Mother
50. Another with same name
52. Casual gathering
55. Hawaiian goose
56. Baseball team
57. Refuse of flax
59. Agricultural implement
63. Conclusion
64. Old age
66. Period of human life
67. Below
68. Argument
69. Beetle
70. Annoying
71. Revise

DOWN
1. Cow flesh
2. Hades
3. Extent of space
4. Hard, silvery white element
5. Acquire
6. Shining brightly
7. Positions
8. Pointed arch
9. Most attractive in a strange way
10. Unlocking implement
11. Brazilian evergreen tree
12. Alert
13. Lakes
18. Lifts
22. Rouses
24. Veterinarian
26. It is
27. Hearing organs
28. Stylish
29. The wood of ebony trees
30. Nut of an oak
34. Public clamor
36. Migrate
37. Situate
39. Overjoy
41. Most domesticated
44. Printer's measures
46. Lair
49. Indehiscent fruit
51. Dissepiment
52. Work dough
53. Language
54. Arm extremities
58. Smell foul
60. Crescent-shaped figure
61. Norse god
62. Direct one's way
64. Dine
65. Anger

Puzzle 59

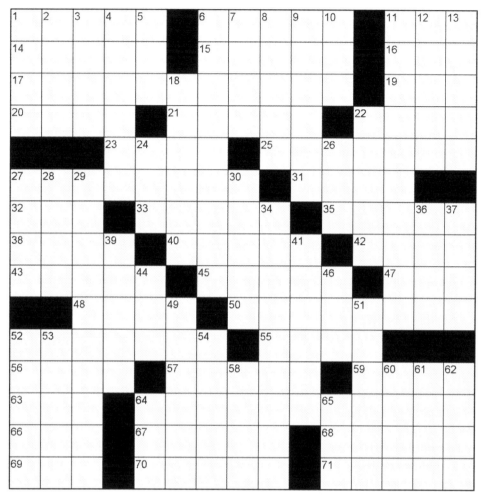

ACROSS
1. Nobleman
6. Relaxed
11. Annoy
14. Long-continued practice
15. Vaguely
16. Pet form of Leonard
17. Feebleness
19. Sheltered side
20. Rice wine
21. Make amends
22. Capital of Fiji
23. Musical composition for one
25. Combed hair
27. Broken pottery fragment
31. Member of mystical Muslim sect
32. Atmosphere
33. Willow
35. Ballroom dance
38. Hit with hand
40. Small drum
42. Reddish brown chalcedony
43. Church council
45. Stratum
47. Small child
48. Predatory sea bird
50. Small baking dishes
52. Very fast (Music)
55. Mother of Apollo
56. Close to
57. French queen, - Antoinette
59. Whimper
63. Pistol
64. Sudden disaster
66. First woman
67. Skilled
68. Notions
69. Captained
70. Curses
71. Verses

DOWN
1. Sprouts
2. At sea
3. Torture device
4. Man-eating woman
5. Born
6. News article
7. Motor car
8. Hurled
9. Church officials
10. Change colour of
11. Persons who claim superior enlightenment
12. Bailiff
13. Mix dough
18. Most wan
22. Divans
24. Exclamation of surprise
26. Not in
27. Succeed in examination
28. Greasy
29. Converted from one language to another
30. Prohibit
34. Supporters of the monarchy
36. Grandmother
37. Probability
39. Card game
41. Bump into again
44. Excavated
46. Soak
49. Battle fleet
51. - dragon, giant monitor lizard
52. Seraph
53. Depart
54. Pertaining to oats
58. Take by force
60. Fencing sword
61. Forcible impact
62. To a smaller extent
64. Taxi
65. Tear

Puzzle 60

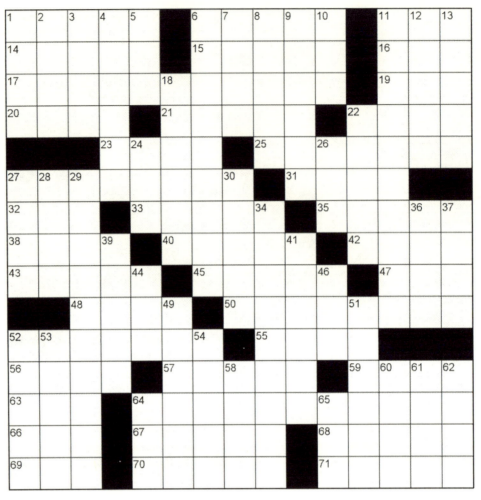

ACROSS
1. Subdue
6. Fronts of ships
11. - de mer, seasickness
14. Unwarranted
15. Eagle's nest
16. Fuss
17. Capable of being addressed
19. Arrest
20. Well-behaved
21. Small islands
22. Insane
23. Skin eruption
25. Widow
27. Small and delicately pretty
31. Title
32. Wrath
33. Lawful
35. The true skin
38. Grandmother
40. Free from gas
42. Monetary unit of Cambodia
43. Mournful sound
45. Refute
47. Vessel built by Noah
48. Marine hazard
50. Ceremonially
52. Goes hungry
55. Mountains
56. Sect
57. Twinned crystal
59. Thrust with a knife
63. Japanese sash
64. Tact
66. Obese
67. Vigorous attack
68. Lubricated
69. Annoying insect
70. Sanity
71. Consecrate

DOWN
1. Quagmire
2. Unwrap
3. Root of the taro
4. Stupid
5. Shelter
6. Fare
7. True
8. Encircled
9. 28th president of the U.S
10. Witness
11. Pertaining to an administrator
12. Maxim
13. Pertaining to a lobe
18. Transgressed
22. Braver
24. Mountain pass
26. Bundle of money
27. Type of fur
28. Republic in SW Asia
29. General principle
30. Enthusiastic
34. Articulate
36. Blackbird
37. An alcoholic
39. Vigilant
41. Victualer
44. Monetary unit of Bulgaria
46. Male sheep
49. Womanly
51. Attack
52. Mock
53. Pertaining to a tube
54. Juniper
58. Infants' beds
60. Roofing item
61. Greek god of war
62. Places to sleep
64. Ethnic telecaster
65. Watch pocket

Puzzle 61

ACROSS
1. Fraud
5. Grotto
9. Disgrace
14. Wheel shaft
15. Spoken
16. Something that consumes
17. Thin
18. Lullaby
20. Bewitch
22. Chemical indicator
23. Greek goddess of the dawn
24. Turbine blade
25. Incessant
30. Talk
33. Coupled
34. Monetary unit of Vietnam
35. Renown
36. Guide
37. Monetary unit of Afghanistan
38. Timid
39. Days before
40. Evil
41. Claim
42. Color
43. Gelatin confection
45. Roster
46. To endure
47. Spatter
50. Tornados
55. Peace of mind
57. Island of Hawaii
58. Shakespearian sprite
59. Machine-gun
60. Above
61. Rush
62. Low-quality diamond
63. Book page

DOWN
1. Robust
2. Beasts of burden
3. Woe is me
4. Prefix, foreign
5. Globular
6. Apprehend
7. South African river
8. Antiquity
9. Having vision
10. Rush
11. Smallest component
12. List of dishes
13. Energy units
19. Grassy plain
21. Reassembled
24. Phial
25. Higher
26. Artless
27. Angered
28. Greek god of love
29. Dull sounds
30. Auctioneer's hammer
31. Spanish, friend
32. Cover with dew
35. Autumn
37. Monetary unit of Yugoslavia
38. Stage shows
40. Public swimming pool
41. Surrounding
43. Mainly
44. Towrope
45. Less common
47. Sovereign
48. South American country
49. Den
50. Polynesian root food
51. Implement
52. Roof overhang
53. Ostrich-like bird
54. Breakers
56. Flow back

Puzzle 62

ACROSS
1. Village
5. Skidded
9. Conceals
14. Off-Broadway theater award
15. First class (1-3)
16. Accustom
17. Fur
18. Deputy regent
20. Canine teeth
22. Affects emotion
23. Beer
24. Gaiter
25. Without exceptions
30. Spun by spiders
33. Tired
34. Feline
35. Rime
36. Ecclesiastical residence
37. Acne pimple
38. To haul with tackle
39. Gaelic
40. Enemy
41. Pressed clothes
42. Poem
43. A fib
45. Indonesian resort island
46. Even (poet.)
47. Fonts
50. Indonesian volcano
55. Flaxseed oil
57. Male swans
58. Change
59. Cain's victim
60. Pipe
61. Sheen
62. Inquisitive
63. Leading player

DOWN
1. Drink to excess
2. Comply
3. Ruse
4. After deductions
5. Savoury sausage
6. Tarry
7. Unit of length
8. Scottish river
9. Wintry
10. Gold bar
11. Musical composition for two
12. Sea eagle
13. Hardens
19. Repatriation (Colloq)
21. Tidal bore
24. Move off hastily
25. Gem cut in relief
26. Bestow
27. Rigid
28. Relax
29. More gelid
30. Stab
31. Artist's support
32. Braid
35. Covering for the head
37. Japanese sandal
38. Edge
40. Untrue
41. Perfectly
43. Becomes narrow
44. Eagles' nests
45. Public transport
47. Metal dross
48. Cultivate
49. Upon
50. Monetary unit of Nigeria
51. Performs
52. Solicit
53. Swedish pop-group of the '70s
54. Consumer
56. Son of Jacob

Puzzle 63

ACROSS
1. Back part of the foot
5. Valley
9. Small rock
14. Potpourri
15. Enough
16. Bower
17. Young salmon
18. Revolts
20. Unfit to be eaten
22. Vent
23. Scottish river
24. Suffix, diminutive
25. Misinterpret
30. Oxlike African antelope
33. Small ring of colour
34. Belonging to him
35. Humble
36. Fats
37. Put on
38. Machete
39. Water
40. Distant
41. Metropolises
42. Outer edge
43. Relative
45. Item of footwear
46. Is able to
47. Peyote
50. Defective pronunciation
55. Climbers staff
57. Taj Mahal site
58. Availing of
59. Migrant farm worker
60. Sob
61. Flood embankment
62. Deceased
63. Stitches

DOWN
1. American Indian
2. Dash
3. Ireland
4. Nobleman
5. Vervain
6. Anoints
7. Roundish projection
8. Female sheep
9. Hail
10. Banal
11. Ancient Greek coin
12. Not one
13. Formerly
19. Waterlily
21. Icons
24. Ireland
25. Of the cheek
26. Inhabitant of Iraq
27. Antitoxin
28. Conclusion
29. Hamlet
30. Arab sprites
31. Desert region in S Israel
32. Edict of the czar
35. Lustreless
37. Matron
38. Keyboard instrument
40. Dupes
41. Broken
43. Alter
44. Wattle tree
45. Vista
47. Handle roughly
48. Otherwise
49. Bludger
50. Half burnt coal
51. Statutes
52. Double curve
53. Developed
54. Yelps
56. Former weight for wool

Puzzle 64

ACROSS
1. Agricultural implement
5. Coarsely ground corn
9. Dismay
14. Long ago
15. Monkeys
16. Twilled cloth
17. Monetary unit of Cambodia
18. Like the lily
20. Put in bondage
22. Decorative cornice
23. Resinous deposit
24. Dowels
25. Dolt
30. Mother
33. Tempt
34. Even (poet.)
35. Wool package
36. Fertilising cell
37. Tree of the genus Quercus
38. Centre of attention
39. Word used in comparisons
40. Minced oath
41. Mountain chain
42. Organ of hearing
43. Divided into seven parts
45. Immature flowers
46. Wine
47. Prostrate
50. Interfering
55. Misdeed
57. 6th month of the Jewish calendar
58. Flower
59. Sky color
60. Cover with wax
61. Type of pie
62. Submachine gun
63. Portable ice-box

DOWN
1. Funeral fire
2. Meat cut
3. Minerals
4. Healthy
5. Save
6. Each
7. Merge
8. Pressure symbol
9. Climb
10. Skins fruit
11. School dance
12. Fever
13. For fear that
19. Of bees
21. Fright
24. Quick glance
25. Class of Indian society
26. 1st letter of the Greek alphabet
27. Blur
28. Incinerate
29. Core
30. Prefix, large
31. Ayers Rock
32. Rocky tablelands
35. An Afrikaner
37. Exclamation of mild dismay
38. Demon
40. Yielded
41. Very small amount
43. Longing for food
44. Boulevard
45. Type of intelligence test
47. Exchange
48. Bear constellation
49. Cooking implements
50. Spleen
51. Ornamental fabric
52. Ancient Roman days
53. Police informer
54. Hoar
56. Observation

Puzzle 65

ACROSS
1. Ground
5. Jute
9. One-celled protozoa
14. Seaward
15. Agave
16. Cogs
17. Prehistoric sepulchral tomb
18. Shaky, clackety old car
20. Right of access over property
22. Cedes
23. Aged
24. Discover
25. Amazing
30. Wood sorrel
33. Carry with great effort
34. Ovum
35. Type of jazz
36. Sturdy
37. Sparse fluid
38. Body fluid
39. Epic poetry
40. Talent
41. Bullfighter
42. Beak
43. Ancient
45. Roseate
46. Furrow
47. Arctic native
50. Eyeglasses
55. Western Australian river flowing into Lake Eyre
57. Tibetan monk
58. Christened
59. A particular
60. Related by blood
61. Ammonia derivative
62. Basic monetary unit of Ghana
63. Arouse

DOWN
1. Openwork fabric
2. Continent
3. Scottish headland
4. An appointment
5. Cleft lip
6. African antelopes
7. Clump of trees
8. Domesticated animal
9. Growing older
10. Measured out
11. British nobleman
12. A nail
13. Egyptian serpents
19. Fibbing
21. Currency
24. Fruit
25. Gray
26. Suffix, view
27. Pulse
28. One's parents (Colloq)
29. Moor
30. Abalone
31. Island in the Bay of Naples
32. Concerned with a specific subject
35. Novice
37. Hoar
38. National gambling game
40. Burning of another's property
41. Earthquake's tidal wave
43. Scent
44. Pressed
45. Covered with hoarfrost
47. Dame - Everage, Humphries' character
48. Thailand
49. Animistic god or spirit
50. Small spider
51. Pottery material
52. Tarn
53. Islamic chieftain
54. Subsided
56. Facial twitch

Puzzle 66

ACROSS
1. Food
5. Pitcher
9. Arrow
14. Ornamental brooch
15. East Indies palm
16. Carved gemstone
17. Network of nerves
18. Agreement reached by three parties
20. Meant for a select few
22. Required
23. Human race
24. Prejudice
25. Lectern in a church
30. Steal from
33. Australian airline
34. Exploit
35. Brief note
36. Naked pictures
37. Play division
38. Potato (Colloq)
39. Stumble
40. Legume
41. Household
42. Dry (wine)
43. Amber-colored candy
45. Food fish
46. Large container
47. Happens
50. Kin
55. Going on
57. Drug-yielding plant
58. Tasmanian river
59. Italian wine province
60. Tears
61. Hits hard
62. Rocky tableland
63. Soviet news service

DOWN
1. Central part
2. Colors
3. Prefix, eight
4. Sharpen
5. Competitor in a contest
6. Fitting with cables
7. Heroic
8. Knock vigorously
9. Screech
10. Loathes
11. Among
12. Festive occasion
13. Having a toe
19. Aniseed
21. Sends out
24. Elite
25. Raves
26. Habituate
27. Early form of sonar
28. Low in pitch
29. Of a Duke
30. Relabel
31. Last letter of the Greek alphabet
32. Wood-eating insect
35. Hindu lawgiver
37. Ethereal
38. Outer coat of a seed
40. Inflect words
41. Pain in the muscles
43. Wood-eating insects
44. Occurrences
45. Gold coin
47. Chooses
48. Bird's crop
49. Unconsciousness
50. Stand
51. Pastry item
52. Hip bones
53. Exclamation of mild dismay
54. Promontory
56. Block up

Puzzle 67

ACROSS
1. Howl
5. Stable attendant
9. Muslim god
14. Double curve
15. Prison room
16. Monetary unit of Sierra Leone
17. One of Columbus's ships
18. Merge
20. Entrapped
22. Worn down
23. Brown shade
24. Daze
25. Peace be with you
30. Droop
33. Greek theatres
34. Drinking vessel
35. Body of organism
36. Grumpy
37. Sweet potato
38. Become ripe
39. Narrow aperture
40. Worthless dog
41. China tea
42. Etcetera
43. Pun
45. Tribe
46. Golf peg
47. Man who flirts with women
50. Ringing in the ears
55. Soften
57. Assess
58. Nasal grunt
59. Greek goddess of the rainbow
60. Way out
61. Saline
62. Employer
63. Serving plate

DOWN
1. Part of skeleton
2. Against
3. Swellings
4. Incline
5. Egyptian beetles
6. Inhabitant of Yemen
7. Dressed
8. Former measure of length
9. Warning bell
10. Citrus fruit
11. A burden
12. Poker stake
13. Have regard
19. Outfit
21. Lack of tone
24. Worthless person
25. Body of deputised hunters
26. Fully developed
27. Adapted to a dry environment
28. Electrical unit
29. Timid
30. Stupor
31. Alter
32. Work groups
35. Grain store
37. Monetary unit of China
38. Aftermath
40. Irish county
41. Unity
43. Ample
44. Inflammation of the ear
45. Flint
47. Fail to hit
48. Old Indian coin
49. Short take-off and landing aircraft
50. Edible tuber
51. Angered
52. Cab
53. Inflammation (Suffix)
54. Third son of Adam
56. Chest bone

Puzzle 68

ACROSS
1. Grant temporary use of
5. Canter
9. Mops
14. 6th month of the Jewish calendar
15. Hick
16. Award of honour
17. Instance
18. Talk in riddles
20. One who leaves to live in another country
22. Made a speech
23. Very skilled person
24. Donations to the poor
25. French national holiday
30. Hallucinogenic drug
33. Agree (to)
34. The (German)
35. Scorch
36. Footwear
37. Bread roll
38. Black and white Chinese animal
39. Dispatch
40. Involuntary muscular contraction
41. Consisting of earth
42. Lyric poem
43. Self-righteous
45. Cormorant
46. Sixth scale note
47. Media chief
50. Shaft fitted with cams
55. Viewing screen of radar equipment
57. Nautical, below
58. Blockade
59. Indigo
60. Climbing plant
61. S-bends
62. Marries
63. Suffix, diminutive

DOWN
1. Ornamental fabric
2. Yellow cheese coated with red wax
3. Malay rice dish, - goreng
4. Small remnant
5. Dark syrup
6. Rivulet
7. Funeral notice
8. Two-year old sheep
9. Ingratiating
10. Scorpion-like N.Z. insect
11. Entrance
12. Basis
13. Toboggan
19. Grinding tooth
21. Incursions
24. Capital of Yemen
25. Bass singer
26. Hurt
27. Small plain cake
28. - off, began golf game
29. Something educed
30. Slow
31. Hindu ascetic
32. Carts
35. Worn by women in India
37. Singer, - Crosby
38. Walkways
40. Lachrymal drops
41. Gives glazed finish to
43. Beaches
44. Venomous snake
45. Theatre platform
47. Scottish Gaelic
48. Speaking platform
49. Roman dates
50. Fruit of the pine
51. Possess
52. Got down from mount
53. Baptismal vessel
54. Affectedly dainty
56. Call of the crow

Puzzle 69

ACROSS
1. Lustreless
5. Fur
9. Skill
14. Opera solo
15. Shakespeare's river
16. Church walkway
17. Water storages
18. 100th anniversary
20. Asleep
22. Bind, esp. to stop bleeding
23. Newt
24. - Christian Andersen
25. Surprising
30. Devoted follower
33. Airplane runway
34. W.A. river
35. Method
36. Standard of perfection
37. Day before
38. Strange and mysterious
39. Fibber
40. Dined
41. Slurred
42. Spread out for drying
43. Containing nitrogen
45. Jester
46. Doctor
47. Constabulary
50. Ready for editing
55. Counts
57. Slew
58. Group of eight
59. Current month
60. Poems
61. Indigent
62. Floor coverings
63. The Occident

DOWN
1. Fathers
2. European mountain range
3. Calcium compound
4. Cut with laser
5. Peaceable
6. Occurrences
7. Lengthy
8. An explosive
9. Punishing
10. Finger ornaments
11. Continent
12. Level
13. Prefix, distant
19. African antelope
21. Of punishment
24. Rent
25. Tilted
26. Cleaning lady
27. Walk
28. - Khayyam
29. Vacillate
30. Do away with
31. Farewell
32. Of necessity
35. Hitler's autobiography, "- Kampf"
37. Suffix, diminutive
38. Choose
40. Artillery sighter
41. Self-important people
43. Subtlety
44. Most peculiar
45. Acted silently
47. Unskilled laborer
48. At one time
49. Stringed instrument
50. Sicilian volcano
51. Confess
52. English monk
53. Dreg
54. Former
56. Intention

Puzzle 70

ACROSS
1. Leave out
5. Title of respect for God
9. Become confused
14. Motor car
15. First king of Israel
16. Hawaiian tree
17. Type of gun
18. Propelling agent
20. Rashness
22. Reigning beauties
23. Metal-bearing mineral
24. Gear wheels
25. Half a semitone
30. Food fish
33. Not read
34. Pigpen
35. Skin opening
36. Land measures
37. New Guinea seaport
38. Small hand drum
39. Dressed
40. Glass container
41. Root vegetable
42. Unlocking implement
43. Instrument for measuring earthquake intensity
45. Toboggan
46. French, water
47. Transfer goods to another boat
50. Large-eyed, Indonesian monkeys
55. Additions
57. Parasitic insect
58. Ghost
59. Gratis
60. Open tart
61. Torridly
62. Fronded plant
63. Arouse

DOWN
1. Kiln for drying hops
2. Silent
3. A particular
4. Pitch
5. Aimed for
6. Bargain
7. Anchored float
8. Peak
9. Claim
10. Valleys
11. Indian pulses
12. Crescent-shaped figure
13. Food
19. Black wood
21. Duty rosters
24. Bird shelter
25. Sound of a duck
26. Male relative
27. Series
28. Marsh plant
29. Russian emperors
30. Venomous snake
31. Lowermost deck
32. Decease
35. Young salmon
37. Put down
38. Spanish river
40. Four-wheel drive vehicles
41. Become coarse
43. Sinuous
44. Stingier
45. Abode of the dead
47. 20th letter of the Hebrew alphabet
48. Public exhibition
49. Springing gait
50. Ripped
51. Full of unresolved questions
52. Australian super-model
53. The back of
54. Subsided
56. If and only if

Puzzle 71

ACROSS
1. Goad
5. Heroin
9. Seaport in SE Scotland
14. One of the divisions of a window
15. Wind instrument
16. Greetings
17. Etching fluid
18. Wind speed measuring instrument
20. Re-examined
22. Disavow
23. New Zealand parrot
24. A clenched hand
25. Realization
30. Vessel or duct
33. State of existing
34. Synthetic yttrium aluminum garnet
35. Crooked
36. Strong cords
37. Needlefish
38. About (Approximate date)
39. Circuits
40. Indian dish
41. Line of police
42. Pig enclosure
43. Travel by railroad
45. Plant having fronds
46. Consume
47. Confront boldly
50. Jeering
55. Science of projectiles
57. Extent of space
58. Inflammatory swelling
59. Continuous dull pain
60. Nipple
61. St - fire (4'1)
62. Lighting gas
63. Serpents

DOWN
1. Mast
2. Tempo
3. Military detachment
4. Advise
5. Noble
6. Wedgelike
7. In bed
8. Leg
9. Most crippled
10. Choose
11. Jot
12. At that time
13. Mature male European red deer
19. Rubber seal (1-4)
21. Short parodies
24. Terror
25. Folds
26. German submarine
27. Having prominent lips
28. Professional charges
29. Australian acacia
30. Italian composer
31. The elbow
32. Smarted
35. Winged creature
37. Secure
38. Raccoonlike carnivore
40. Pub game
41. Become coarse
43. Tree exudations
44. Resound
45. Book leaf
47. French clergyman
48. Summon
49. Large mollusc
50. Cube
51. Information
52. Angers
53. Tides that attain the least height
54. Guns (Slang)
56. Convert into leather

Puzzle 72

ACROSS
1. River of Hades
5. Bushman's pack
9. 3 Chums
14. School dance
15. Spouse
16. Asunder
17. Wrinkle
18. Utterly unyielding
20. Sycophant
22. Esophagus
23. Fish part
24. Breezy
25. Reliable
30. Sack
33. Free of an obstruction
34. Scottish river
35. Japanese wrestler
36. European ermine
37. Rodent
38. Prefix, turbine
39. Tartan skirt
40. Cheer
41. Snake sounds
42. Sorrowful
43. Worship of demons
45. High-pitched tone
46. Advanced in years
47. Moneychanger
50. Line left by ocean on shore
55. Peace of mind
57. Soon
58. Shakespearian sprite
59. Machine-gun
60. Bristle
61. Covered with mold
62. Manager
63. Exchange

DOWN
1. Agile
2. Authentic
3. System of meditation
4. Christmas
5. Teetering
6. Broadens
7. From a distance
8. Jewel
9. Fertiliser
10. Fittingly
11. Appendage
12. Sea eagle
13. Let it stand
19. Spry
21. Astir
24. Encourage in wrongdoing
25. Teething biscuits
26. Abstract beings
27. Berate
28. Plot of ground
29. State in the NW United States
30. Explode
31. Yellowish brown color
32. Like a goose
35. Ruined city in W Iran
37. Sloping walkway
38. Diacritic
40. Marine hazards
41. Australian cars
43. Dexterously
44. Sounds
45. Drilled
47. Bogus
48. Champion
49. Train track
50. Polynesian root food
51. Church service
52. Once more
53. Roster
54. Summit of a small hill
56. Wane

Puzzle 73

ACROSS
1. Category
5. Molten rock
9. Splash through mud
14. Hip bones
15. Ebony
16. Fencing leap
17. Enclosure for skating arena
18. Dish for salt
20. Sideways
22. Puts at rest
23. Fish eggs
24. Takes a seat
25. Reason for being (6.1'4)
30. Indicate assent
33. Torpedo vessels (1-5)
34. Large barrel
35. Starch used in puddings
36. Walk crab-like
37. Besides
38. Lapwing
39. Prepare for publication
40. Exclamation of surprise
41. Cling
42. Cardinal number
43. Supple arms and legs
45. Mother of Jesus
46. Scottish river
47. Endeavour
50. Superior quality
55. Redeploy
57. Pierce with horn
58. Inward feeling
59. Shakespeare's river
60. Egg-shaped
61. Church official
62. A man
63. Gape

DOWN
1. Father
2. Fetid
3. Circular band
4. Steal
5. Sores
6. Humiliated
7. Rodent
8. Social insect
9. Slender
10. Lounges
11. Earthen pot
12. Remain
13. Possessive pronoun
19. Pile of stones
21. Put pen to paper
24. Breeding horse
25. Readjust
26. Live
27. Halogen element
28. Preservative
29. Alcohol burners
30. Governor in Mogul India
31. Pointed arch
32. Was foolishly fond of
35. Appear
37. Nautical call
38. Worked at
40. Major artery
41. Lenient
43. Bigger
44. US electronics inventor, Thomas -
45. International code
47. Gaelic
48. Examine by touch
49. Loving
50. Jitterbug
51. Highly excited
52. Bright star
53. Sketch
54. Shrill bark
56. Henpeck

Puzzle 74

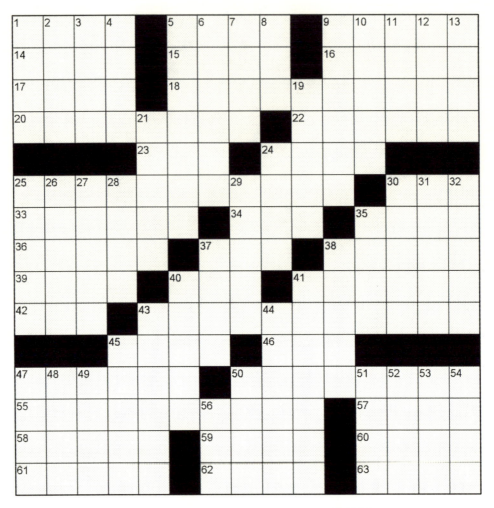

ACROSS
1. Liberate
5. Mimicked
9. Crawled
14. Jot
15. Kill
16. Proportion
17. Commonsense
18. Leader
20. Fickle
22. Boggy
23. Limb
24. Be sorry for
25. Measuring tool (4.7)
30. Small child
33. Related
34. Everything
35. Shrub
36. River in W Canada
37. Beer
38. - voce, in a low tone
39. Migrant farm worker
40. Optic organ
41. Performer on ice
42. - Kelly
43. Detailed inspection
45. Wealthy
46. Decay
47. Formally withdraw
from
50. Painfulness
55. Propelling agent
57. Killer whale
58. Inquirer
59. Double curve
60. Crack
61. Spins
62. Division of a hospital
63. Garment edges

DOWN
1. Fish appendages
2. Black bird
3. Sewing case
4. The Orient
5. Aimed for
6. Blood fluid
7. Every
8. Coloring material
9. Make
10. Infested with vermin
11. Suffix, diminutive
12. Jetty
13. Member of the Conservative Party
19. Eddy
21. Domesticated
24. Whimper
25. Claw
26. Similar
27. Tartan
28. Ireland
29. American witch hunt city
30. All (mus.)
31. Prefix, bone
32. Rose prickle
35. Water craft
37. Indian nursemaid
38. Perform on ice
40. Surpass
41. Grunted
43. Downy ducks
44. Clothes presser
45. Repulse
47. Stout pole
48. Scottish Gaelic
49. Half burnt coal
50. Heroic story
51. Food
52. Sea eagle
53. Confidence trick
54. Undermines
56. Base

Puzzle 75

ACROSS
1. Crazy
5. Charge per unit
9. Animate
14. Gemstone
15. Reflected sound
16. Nimble
17. Persian fairy
18. Destroyer of images
20. Backer
22. Ice ax
23. Donkey
24. Lotto-like gambling game
25. Suspecting
30. Prefix, over
33. Meal course
34. Abstract being
35. Wax
36. Less contaminated
37. Exclamation of surprise
38. Prospered
39. Salver
40. Terminal digit of the foot
41. Nation in N North America
42. Chop
43. Charitable donation
45. Measure of medicine
46. Malt beverage
47. Disallowed bowling delivery in cricket (2-4)
50. Dancers' one-peice costumes
55. Corrective
57. Book of the Bible
58. Tranquillity
59. Off-Broadway theater award
60. Title of respect for God
61. Go into
62. Noble
63. Pause

DOWN
1. Easy stride
2. Candid
3. Comic person
4. Potpourri
5. Distribute again
6. Right to enter
7. Norse god of thunder
8. An age
9. Thrashing
10. Eskimo dwelling
11. Glass bottle
12. Otherwise
13. After deductions
19. Unfolds
21. Less common
24. Basic currency of Papua New Guinea
25. Distance downwards
26. Habituate
27. Dry stalks
28. Three (Cards)
29. Snicker
30. Caravansary
31. Hives
32. Earthwork
35. Tilt
37. First-class
38. Gem surface
40. Unit of magnetic induction
41. Monk of the Eastern Church
43. More daring
44. Fairy
45. Move to music
47. Back of neck
48. Augury
49. Vanquish
50. Ear part
51. Slightly open
52. Cloak
53. Debutantes
54. Narrow strip of wood
56. Summit

Puzzle 76

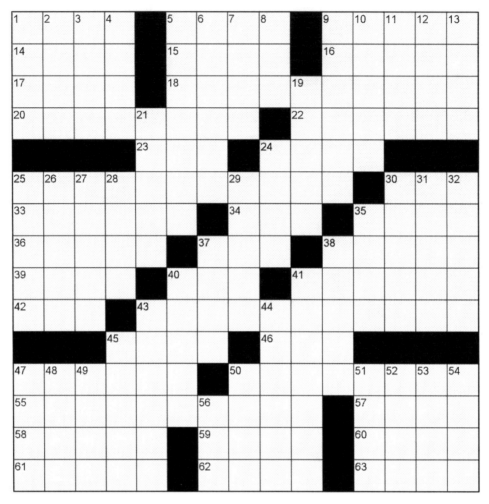

ACROSS
1. Sturdy wool fiber
5. Russian parliament before 1917
9. Got up
14. Skin eruption
15. Mild oath
16. Rod used to reinforce concrete
17. Natter
18. Scorching
20. Horny
22. Joins
23. Crude mineral
24. Obstacle
25. Dispirits
30. Prefix, over
33. Book of the Bible
34. Sunbeam
35. Persian fairy
36. Hood-like membranes
37. Norse goddess
38. Worries
39. Diplomacy
40. Tibetan ox
41. Covered passage
42. Very skilled person
43. Harassment
45. Incline
46. Terminal digit of the foot
47. Neat
50. Grecian
55. Nutritive
57. Alter
58. Person that loses
59. Wife of one's uncle
60. Egyptian goddess of fertility
61. Paradises
62. Exultation
63. Catalog

DOWN
1. Torture device
2. Continuous dull pain
3. Growl
4. Japanese wooden clog
5. Prophetess of Israel
6. More gruesome
7. Female servant
8. Commercials
9. Stadia
10. Set up again
11. Funeral notice
12. Sensible
13. Work units
19. Tuna
21. New Guinea currency units
24. Authenticating mark
25. Judicial rulings
26. Son of Abraham
27. Gravy
28. Sword handle
29. Arduous journeys
30. Caravansary
31. Hives
32. Ascended
35. Agreement
37. Stringed instrument
38. Sadistic
40. Republic in S Arabia
41. Novice
43. Persons setting the speed
44. Eternal (Poet)
45. Cud
47. An auction
48. Walk wearily
49. Stand
50. Drag
51. Wicked
52. Malay rice dish, - goreng
53. Greek goddess of the rainbow
54. Wen
56. Label

Puzzle 77

ACROSS
1. Italian currency
5. Murky
9. Concerning
14. Enough
15. Malarial fever
16. Book leaf
17. Suffix, diminutive
18. Vindictively
20. Wine variety
22. Washes out
23. Eccentric
24. Rowing implements
25. An imperial system of government
30. Corded cloth
33. Ancient Mexican
34. Malt beverage
35. Nil
36. Ways out
37. Missus
38. Musical endings
39. Small rodents
40. Mire
41. Clause
42. Large body of water
43. Wise guy
45. - Disney
46. Land measure
47. Relaxing
50. Almond-flavored liqueur
55. Tedious jobs
57. Food
58. New
59. Doing nothing
60. Lout
61. Conscious
62. Turkish governors
63. Food scraps

DOWN
1. Sly look
2. Monetary unit of Peru
3. Routine
4. Inspires dread
5. Pertaining to the Biblical David
6. Plan
7. Ladder step
8. Beer barrel
9. Uphold
10. Proper words
11. Old cloth measures
12. African river
13. Playthings
19. Rub out
21. Traditions
24. Lubricates
25. Articles
26. Verve
27. Fold
28. Suffix, diminutive
29. Immense
30. Barricade river again
31. Rub out
32. Difficult question
35. Japanese sandal
37. The majority
38. Applaud
40. Ship bottom
41. Clauses
43. Contrive through trickery
44. That is to say
45. Broader
47. Dame - Everage, Humphries' character
48. In a line
49. Fijian capital
50. Assistant
51. Reflected sound
52. Norse god of thunder
53. Trumpet sound
54. 3 Admits
56. Chest bone

Puzzle 78

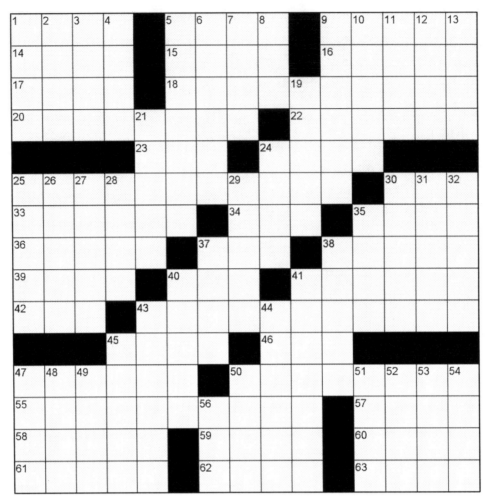

ACROSS
1. Morning
5. Flutter
9. Small round shield
14. Notion
15. Entrance
16. Perfect
17. Flesh
18. Laws
20. Marriage
22. Lie down
23. Hard-shelled fruit
24. Category
25. Bladder worm
30. Ethnic telecaster
33. Recaptured
34. Not in
35. Gael
36. Full speed
37. Find the sum of
38. Vampire
39. Shroud
40. Female deer
41. Travelling on
42. Finish
43. Asexual reproduction
45. Fluster
46. Monkey
47. Become a pupa
50. Sloping
55. Stems from
57. Indian nursemaid
58. Greek theatre
59. Rave
60. Father
61. Desires
62. Nestling
63. Formerly

DOWN
1. Act silently
2. Lyric poems
3. Harvest
4. Western pact
5. Alas
6. Congenitally attached
7. Glass bottle
8. Etcetera
9. Stopwatches
10. Skilled
11. City in W Nevada
12. Guns (Slang)
13. Otherwise
19. Freshwater game fish
21. Federation
24. Driving shower
25. Yearn
26. Arab country
27. Sober
28. Work hard
29. Cowboy exhibition
30. Lead ups to finals
31. Small yeast-raised pancake
32. Male deer
35. Juniper
37. First-class
38. Napery
40. Twelve
41. Feasts
43. Morning church service
44. Principal ore of lead
45. Bundle of sticks
47. Small pond
48. Official language of Pakistan
49. Pastry items
50. Remain
51. Record conversation
52. 8th month of the Jewish calendar
53. Sleeps briefly
54. Steps descending to a river
56. Part of verb to be

Puzzle 79

ACROSS
1. Dry watercourse
5. Stratagem
9. Huge
14. Potpourri
15. Towards the centre
16. Slender boat
17. Cheat the system
18. Most crunchy
20. Separated
22. Husky
23. Greek letter
24. Piebald
25. Disbelieved
30. Girl (Slang)
33. Worshipper
34. Indian dish
35. Martial art
36. Breathes rattlingly
37. Scale note
38. Female servants
39. Melt
40. Monetary unit of Afghanistan
41. Feudal tax
42. Male child
43. Tenant under a lease
45. Carbonized fuel
46. Russian community
47. Mock
50. Proved
55. Hatefulness
57. Sprint contest
58. Leers
59. Redact
60. Taj Mahal site
61. Rent out again
62. Not difficult
63. High roll of hair

DOWN
1. Part of speech
2. Drug-yielding plant
3. Grime
4. Jot
5. Earthquake scale
6. Not perused
7. Collar fastener
8. Long period of time
9. Reverberated
10. Nymph presiding over rivers
11. Unique thing
12. Antarctic explorer
13. Allot
19. Lad
21. Roman goddess of agriculture
24. Egyptian deity
25. Pub game
26. State in the NW United States
27. Gannet
28. Ship's company
29. Objects of worship
30. Corporation
31. Muddle
32. The one defeated
35. Prison
37. Twofold
38. New Zealand aboriginal
40. Alps
41. Craving a drink
43. Grasshopper
44. Vomiting
45. Bush call
47. Dull person
48. Brink
49. Grain factory
50. The sacred scriptures of Hinduism
51. Bind securely (Nautical)
52. The villain in Othello
53. Colour of unbleached linen
54. Unhearing
56. Born

Puzzle 80

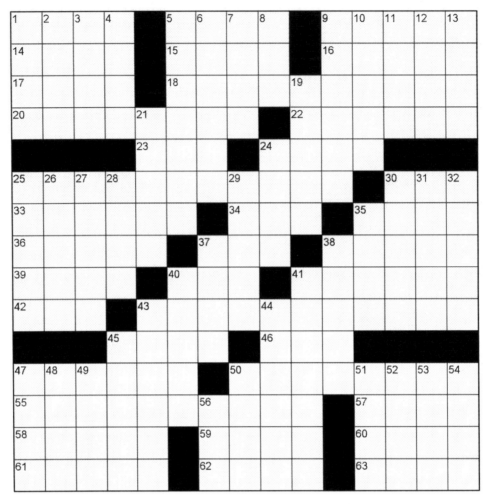

ACROSS
1. Yawn
5. Mould
9. Derision
14. Chilled
15. Double curve
16. Cautious
17. Amphibian
18. Grounds where the "Sport of Kings" are held
20. Apartment house
22. Australian airline
23. Aged
24. American Indian
25. Coffee makers
30. Garment edge
33. Exaggerate
34. Cattle fodder
35. Jet-assisted takeoff
36. Oriental peanut sauce
37. Unit of loudness
38. Combat
39. Dutch cheese
40. Crow call
41. If it be so
42. Corded cloth
43. Sequel
45. Monetary unit of Italy
46. Firearm
47. Reverberates
50. Migraine
55. Constant
57. Photograph of bones (1-3)
58. Scope
59. Profane expression
60. Loch
61. Incites
62. Donkey call
63. Female sheep

DOWN
1. Present
2. Land measure
3. Unskilled laborer
4. Brink
5. Sour cherry
6. Republic in E Africa
7. Denomination
8. Golfers mound
9. Small plain cakes
10. Bring about
11. Barbarous person
12. Repose
13. Russian no
19. Tote
21. Melancholic
24. Ember
25. Difficult question
26. Avoid
27. Rap with fingers again
28. Pack fully
29. Muscles
30. City in W Germany
31. Moral code
32. Clump of trees
35. Zigzag before the wind (Yachting)
37. Small yeast cake
38. Located
40. Damn
41. Pulpy
43. Blockades
44. Excrement
45. Rope used to guide a horse
47. Beige
48. Burn slightly
49. Drape
50. Listen to
51. Wheel shaft
52. Bird's crop
53. Codlike fish
54. Sight organs
56. To hit a ball high

Puzzle 81

ACROSS
1. Accompanied by
5. Congeal
9. Bewitch
14. Melody
15. Death rattle
16. Hebrew prophet
17. Serene
18. Leaving to live in another country
20. Unequal
22. Salt of oleic acid
23. Lair
24. Scottish Celt
25. Engagement
30. Small bird
33. Small galley
34. Printer's measures
35. Cap of Scottish origin
36. Scottish, concerning
37. Vessel or duct
38. Dry red wine
39. Alp
40. Spasm
41. Car shed
42. Antiquity
43. Cowardly
45. Relaxation
46. Beer
47. Close-fitting dress
50. Hotel manager
55. Twill-weave woolen cloth
57. French novelist
58. Incites
59. Consumer
60. Projecting edge
61. Stop prematurely
62. Simpleton
63. Poker stake

DOWN
1. City in central Texas
2. Republic in SW Asia
3. Roofing slate
4. Poor actors
5. Credible
6. Mourn
7. Fetid
8. Two-year old sheep
9. Ski lodge
10. Hostelry
11. Largest continent
12. Hire
13. Magician
19. Brown and white horses
21. Stupid person
24. Jewels
25. Wide open
26. Jury
27. Beg
28. Hog sound
29. Pithy
30. Tasmanian river
31. Icon
32. Flirted
35. Weight allowance
37. Objectionable
38. Auctioneer's hammer
40. Dubious
41. Unit of magnetomotive force
43. Most up to date
44. Bay tree
45. Soother
47. Predatory sea bird
48. Medicinal plant
49. Therefore
50. Mexican currency
51. Log house of rural Russia
52. Maize
53. Got down from mount
54. Title
56. Mire

Puzzle 82

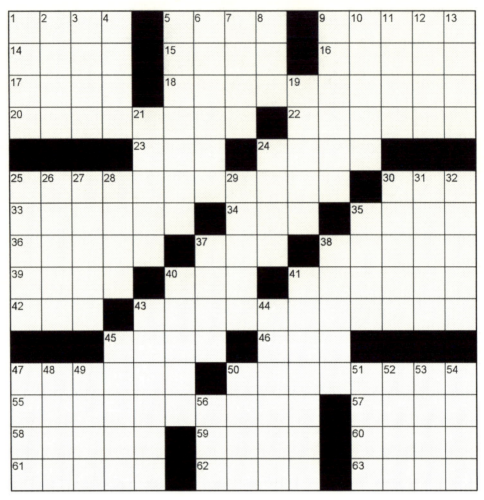

ACROSS
1. Cook in oven
5. Rabble
9. German dive bomber
14. Pitcher
15. Australian super-model
16. Sharpened
17. Temple
18. Liberal
20. Antiutopia
22. Grain fungi
23. A swelling
24. Prayer
25. Not joined
30. Government broadcaster
33. Nervousness
34. Hurried
35. Frizzy hair style
36. Belief
37. Exclamation of disgust
38. Change
39. Vow
40. Turkish headwear
41. Revere
42. Energy
43. Pun
45. Wife of Jacob
46. Bleat
47. Adventurous expedition
50. Scraps
55. Beekeeping
57. Harvest
58. Small spiders
59. Ancient Greek coin
60. Festive occasion
61. Out of date
62. Lairs
63. Candid

DOWN
1. Curve
2. Apart
3. Greek island in the Aegean
4. Former
5. Begins negotiations again
6. Pertaining to the Alps
7. Parasitic insect
8. Marsh
9. Divided evenly
10. South-Western Pacific island kingdom
11. Untie
12. Young guinea fowl
13. Appends
19. Trojan beauty
21. Possessed
24. Egyptian deity
25. Remove a cap
26. Impertinence
27. Crawl
28. Finished
29. Insane
30. Later
31. Propagate
32. Bulb-like stems
35. Singer
37. Yes
38. Dam extending across the Nile
40. Thresh
41. Gives glazed finish to
43. Read
44. Fairy king
45. Shoestrings
47. Coarsely ground corn
48. Capital of Western Samoa
49. Seizures
50. Hick
51. Jason's ship
52. Lowest high tide
53. Story
54. Duration
56. Fox

Puzzle 83

ACROSS
1. Garment of ancient Rome
5. Inhabitant of Denmark
9. Orchid plant drug
14. Ugly growth
15. Egg
16. Winged
17. State of USA
18. Kneels
20. Quell
22. Small case worn on chain around neck
23. Breakfast cereal
24. Sticky stuffs
25. Laborious work
30. Total
33. Ill-treats
34. Antiquity
35. Left
36. Customs
37. New Zealand parrot
38. Small animals
39. Young salmon
40. Information
41. Seaport in N France
42. Pigpen
43. Predatory mammal
45. Coral islands
46. Headwear
47. Matching set of jewels
50. Interpretations
55. Types of trees, particularly pines
57. Minor oath
58. Leave undisturbed (3.2)
59. Starchy food grain
60. Undergo lysis
61. Gorge
62. Small secluded valley
63. Egress

DOWN
1. Pairs
2. Island of Hawaii
3. Clench
4. On the top
5. Turns down corner of page to mark place (3-4)
6. Zoroaster bible
7. Cloistered women
8. Large flightless bird
9. Main ship's cabin
10. Smart - , show-offs
11. Shortage
12. Suffix, diminutive
13. Nuisance
19. Inundate
21. Gowns
24. Venomous lizard
25. Torches
26. German submarine (1-4)
27. Hot dish
28. A person that uses
29. Adolescent years
30. Underwater navigational aid
31. Undo
32. Untidy
35. Swallow
37. New Zealand parrots
38. Floating platforms
40. Renee -, Australian rock singer
41. Become coarse
43. Canal boats
44. From that time
45. Restrains
47. Money
48. Affirm with confidence
49. Network of nerves
50. Face concealment
51. Lazy
52. Large African antelope
53. Malay rice dish, - goreng
54. Printer's mark, keep
56. Work unit

Puzzle 84

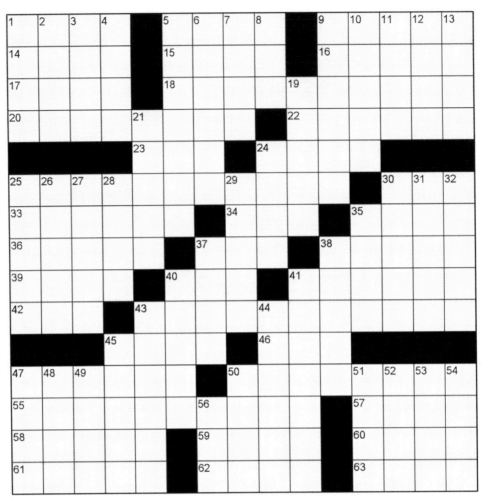

ACROSS
1. Jest
5. Sweetheart
9. Wake up
14. Heroic
15. Line of revolution
16. Enemy aviator
17. 9th letter of the Hebrew alphabet
18. Burial grounds
20. Students
22. Conundrum
23. Last month
24. Relations
25. Enduring
30. Fairy queen
33. Ancient Greek god
34. Primate
35. Diminish
36. Rocky tablelands
37. Missus
38. Vacillate
39. Reared
40. Sum charged
41. Losing colour
42. Morose
43. Authorities on Greek and Roman studies
45. Skidded
46. Writing fluid
47. Lure
50. More drowsy
55. Exaggerates
57. Tibetan monk
58. Skin disease of animals
59. Swellings
60. Against
61. Large tree
62. Suffix, diminutive
63. Misdeed

DOWN
1. Fast planes
2. Oil cartel
3. - and kin (Friends and relations)
4. Reverberate
5. Codfish
6. Brings to bear
7. Intentions
8. Avail of
9. Growing older
10. Language elements
11. Among
12. Yacht stabiliser
13. Scottish Gaelic
19. Triple
21. Temporary stillnesses
24. Two-up bats
25. Young sheep
26. Musical drama
27. Nuzzled
28. Delighted
29. Vetches
30. Song thrush
31. Concerning
32. South African mountains
35. Dry riverbed
37. Alcoholic drink of fermented honey
38. Poorly sorted sandstone
40. Sparking stone
41. Skill
43. Nearer
44. Mute
45. Twilled cloth
47. Prolonged unconsciousness
48. Egg-shaped
49. Set right
50. Let it stand
51. Plot of ground
52. The villain in Othello
53. Islamic chieftain
54. Rave
56. Reverential fear

Puzzle 85

ACROSS
1. Spurt
5. Demonstrative pronoun
9. Wane
14. Region
15. Advise
16. Hue
17. Medicine tablet
18. Sandy
20. Hatching of a larva
22. Cylindrical
23. Beer
24. Jumps on one leg
25. Increasing in heat
30. Domesticated animal
33. Made of different-color fibers
34. Pewter
35. Dam
36. At right angles to a ships length
37. Petroleum
38. Gambling game
39. Leaves
40. Raincoat
41. Dog's shelter
42. Observation
43. Woman who works
45. Freshwater fish
46. Dove sound
47. Think
50. Reads to a stenographer
55. Male turkey
57. Be foolishly fond of
58. Interior
59. Doing nothing
60. Poker stake
61. Shabby
62. Performer
63. Unpleasant smell

DOWN
1. Stare with open mouth
2. Of urine
3. Vend
4. Nimbus
5. Followed behind
6. Champions
7. Capital of Yemen
8. Decade
9. Receive
10. South Africans
11. Drug-yielding plant
12. Advertise boastfully
13. Gaelic
19. Lack of tone
21. American witch hunt city
24. Foot part
25. Idealized concept of a loved one
26. Influential person
27. American Indians
28. Exclamation to express sorrow
29. Slight sharp sound
30. Monetary unit of Finland
31. Swiss mountain
32. Scandinavian mythical demon
35. Flying limb
37. Rowing implements
38. Procreated
40. Saunter
41. One that knocks
43. Boggy
44. Tapering mass of ice
45. Cooked in oven
47. Inflammation (Suffix)
48. Sand hill
49. Sea eagle
50. Extinct flightless bird
51. 6th month of the Jewish calendar
52. Pitch
53. Suffix, diminutive
54. Search
56. Spanish hero

Puzzle 86

ACROSS
1. Store
5. Lazy
9. Make watertight
14. Periodic movement of the sea
15. Sound of a cat
16. - Welles, actor, producer, and director
17. Related by blood
18. Strong-flavored cheese
20. Delivered
22. Funeral car
23. Groove
24. Red planet
25. Link together
30. Mineral spring
33. Excite
34. Legal right
35. Twosomes
36. Saltpetre
37. Colorful form of the common carp
38. Garlic-flavored mayonnaise
39. - off, began golf game
40. Beetle
41. Hemoglobin deficiency
42. Aged
43. The act of subdividing
45. Emperor of Rome

54-68
46. 13th letter of the Hebrew alphabet
47. Destroyer
50. Sprawl
55. Merry-go-round
57. State in the central United States
58. Elegance
59. Verge
60. Departs
61. Finished
62. Come to ground
63. Struck

DOWN
1. Celestial body
2. Long walk
3. Norse god
4. Remain undecided
5. Sink to the level of a brute
6. Erase
7. Noisy
8. Female sheep
9. Stick together
10. Regions
11. A person that uses
12. Profit failure
13. Leg joint
19. Natters
21. Efface
24. Island in central Hawaii
25. Division of a long poem
26. Bay window
27. Eminent
28. Coagulated milk
29. Norse god of winds
30. Finnish name of Finland
31. Infantile paralysis
32. Indian or Chinese
35. Ceases living
37. Monetary unit of Nigeria
38. Soul
40. Indian millet
41. Warded off
43. Sowed
44. Cast doubt upon
45. Time being
47. Incite
48. Scandinavian Fate
49. Couple
50. Alkali
51. Excavates
52. Fate
53. Monetary unit of Angola
54. The Orient
56. Ten decibels

Puzzle 87

ACROSS
1. Helsinki citizen
5. Hood-like membrane
9. Frighten
14. Agave
15. Monster
16. Watered garden
17. Coin
18. Repeated
20. External
22. Conform to city habits
23. - Vegas, US gambling city
24. Old cloth measures
25. Navy officer
30. Taxicab
33. Not done
34. Ignited
35. 11th letter of the Hebrew alphabet
36. Hair net
37. Affirmative reply
38. Elastic material
39. Lawn
40. French, water
41. Silent movies star, Buster -
42. Transgress
43. Climaxing
45. Shave
46. Policeman
47. Gambling house
50. Australian state
55. Climbers staff
57. Hoarfrost
58. Condiment
59. Ruse
60. Distant
61. Made a mistake
62. River in central Europe
63. Demonstration

DOWN
1. Visage
2. Holly
3. Something not to be done (2-2)
4. After deductions
5. Abrade
6. Prejudice against old people
7. Of urine
8. Permit
9. Strident
10. Outer garments
11. Italian wine province
12. Marine hazard
13. Whirlpool
19. Applause
21. African antelope
24. Greek goddess of strife
25. Oxidises
26. Boredom
27. Decorate
28. House top
29. Lower portion of the small intestine
30. Desert plants
31. Worn to protect the clothing
32. Cannabis
35. Monetary unit of Burma
37. American university
38. Jumped
40. Wallaroos
41. Door striker
43. Preserved in a can
44. Tapering mass of ice
45. A bit
47. Instance
48. Having wings
49. Goad
50. Empty
51. Toward the mouth
52. Prevalent
53. Officiating priest of a mosque
54. Air (prefix)
56. A couple

Puzzle 88

ACROSS
1. In the greatest number
5. Israeli round dance
9. Slop over
14. Hip bones
15. Spoken
16. Lofty nest
17. Lustrous fur
18. Petty fault finding
20. Sideways
22. Plumes
23. Monetary unit of Vietnam
24. Ceases living
25. Tricorn
30. Which person
33. Monetary unit of Saudi Arabia
34. Needlefish
35. Infant's carriage
36. Useful
37. Upper limb
38. Fishing net
39. Clock face
40. Supplement
41. Capital of Massachusetts
42. Turf
43. Parrot fever
45. Boatswain
46. Former measure of length
47. Frolic
50. Bonfire
55. Peace of mind
57. Frown
58. Shakespearian sprite
59. Wrongfully assist
60. Inspires dread
61. Marshy
62. Clarets
63. Created

DOWN
1. Jester
2. Fetid
3. Carol
4. Grasp
5. Capital of the Solomon Islands
6. Prayer
7. Assess
8. Peak
9. Holy
10. Small dogs
11. Eye part
12. Cotton fibre
13. Limbs
19. More gelid
21. Intact
24. Small drink of liquor
25. Dull sounds
26. Rate
27. Greek epic poem
28. Cry out
29. Heron
30. Subpoenas
31. Capital of Vietnam
32. Portents
35. Mexican currency
37. Related
38. Plinth
40. S-bends
41. Dramatic dances
43. Corpulent
44. Tormented
45. Made a hole
47. Fraud
48. Republic in W South America
49. Put down
50. Small child
51. Drumbeat
52. U.S. State
53. Regretted
54. Scottish Gaelic
56. Otic organ

Puzzle 89

ACROSS
1. Grove
5. Small blemish
9. Animal
14. Nautical, below
15. State in the central United States
16. Wireless
17. Agave
18. Make slender
20. Gambler
22. Raved
23. U-turn (Colloq)
24. Untidy state
25. Farthest west
30. Monetary unit of Burma
33. Evades
34. Public transport
35. Thick slice
36. Dipper
37. Falsehood
38. Serpentine
39. Redact
40. Minced oath
41. Surprises
42. Not sweet
43. Gymnastic event for women
45. Knitting stitch
46. Exclamation of surprise
47. Guarantee
50. A case of a runny nose
55. Without ardor
57. Helper
58. Analyze a sentence
59. Separate article
60. Tidy
61. Charger
62. Levels of karate proficiency
63. Mouth parts

DOWN
1. Dutch name of The Hague
2. Earthen pot
3. Appear threateningly
4. Affectedly dainty
5. Female siblings
6. Armor for the knee
7. One who is indebted
8. Brown shade
9. Bosom
10. Works for
11. Entrance
12. Dimensions
13. Having pedal digits
19. Clothe
21. Soft leather
24. Pouting grimace
25. Part of Great Britain
26. Elude
27. Containing sodium
28. Lean
29. African musical instrument
30. Put
31. Work
32. An abyss
35. Scorning person
37. Recline in a relaxed manner
38. Bundle of cereal plants
40. Mark of omission
41. Divisions
43. Interred
44. Norwegian arctic explorer
45. Money bag
47. Egyptian serpents
48. Gaiter
49. Father
50. Bristle
51. Tooth
52. Stead
53. Yellow cheese coated with red wax
54. Hardens
56. Bottle top

Puzzle 90

ACROSS
1. Lethargic
5. Off-Broadway theater award
9. Baccarat term
14. Extent of space
15. Bog
16. Negatively charged ion
17. Prison room
18. Having a constant entropy
20. Concentrated extracts
22. Challenge again
23. Part of a circle
24. Challenge
25. The state of being omnipotent
30. Also
33. Virgin
34. Tibetan ox
35. Entreaty
36. Sea eagles
37. Piece
38. Condescend
39. Obtains
40. Heavy weight
41. Fruit ice
42. Fire remains
43. Reproductive
45. Hired thug
46. Covered vehicle
47. Rise
50. Involving surgery
55. Halt
57. Garden tool
58. Black tea
59. Gaelic
60. Ireland
61. Lance
62. - off, began golf game
63. Dint

DOWN
1. Openwork fabric
2. Crude minerals
3. Sets
4. American university
5. 15th letter of the Greek alphabet
6. Halve
7. Angers
8. Even (poet.)
9. Sheer fabric
10. Battery terminal
11. East Indies palm
12. Coconut husk fibre
13. At one time
19. Trail
21. Backs of necks
24. Biting insect
25. Last letter of the Greek alphabet
26. Female horses
27. Coming between 8 and 10
28. Ancient Roman days
29. Watching
30. Elsewhere excuse
31. Desert region in S Israel
32. "Inferno" author
35. Saucy
37. Benefit
38. Performing
40. Canters
41. Growled
43. 3 Ruminate
44. Extract forcibly
45. Spinnaker-like sail
47. Serpents
48. Pace
49. Shaped mass of food
50. Male parent
51. Angered
52. Attention
53. Related by blood
54. Time of abstinence
56. 9th letter of the Hebrew alphabet

Puzzle 91

ACROSS
1. Twinned crystal
6. Untidy person
10. Log house of rural Russia
14. Eskimo
15. Slay
16. Mend socks
17. Compass point
18. Unwrap
19. In bed
20. Provokation
23. Greeting
24. Long period of time
25. Comes out
27. Bridge over another road
32. Spiritual part of a human
33. Transfix
34. Say
36. Whinny
39. Employs
41. Smarted
43. Apportion
44. Hindu garments
46. Sprites
48. Hard-shelled fruit
49. Glimpse
51. Canine teeth
53. Device for cooling
56. Monetary unit of Japan
57. Possesses
58. Overstates
64. Roman poet
66. Notion
67. Idealized concept of a loved one
68. Lotto-like gambling game
69. Tilt
70. Regional
71. Work units
72. Minerals
73. Become eroded

DOWN
1. Short dress
2. Soon
3. Worthless dogs
4. Rubbish
5. Abyssinians
6. Predatory sea bird
7. Bits of thread
8. A parent
9. Blossoms
10. Highest mountain in Crete
11. Custardlike dessert
12. Mark placed over a vowel
13. South American mountains
21. Biting insects
22. Lighting gas
26. Regretted
27. Literary work
28. Entry permit
29. Giving energy to
30. Cloy
31. Musty
35. Covetousness
37. Surfeit
38. 8th letter of the Hebrew alphabet
40. Window ledge
42. Farm birds
45. Flat-fish
47. Uncontaminated
50. Republic in S North America
52. Captivate
53. Strangle
54. Vacillate
55. Navigational aid
59. Hereditary factor
60. Guns (Slang)
61. Savoury Mexican dish
62. Mild oath
63. Flat-fish
65. - and don'ts

Puzzle 92

ACROSS
1. Fop
6. Score
10. Pile
14. Fail at a premature stage
15. Church recess
16. Upon
17. Undertake (an examination) after having previously failed it
18. Openings
19. Suffix, diminutive
20. Make ethereal
23. Male sheep
24. Akin
25. Incense burner
27. Full of twists
32. Proper word
33. Mature
34. Insane
36. Witchcraft
39. Units of loudness
41. Giant
43. Melt
44. Oozes
46. Small round shield
48. Day before
49. Feminine name
51. Recompensed
53. Spinning wheel
56. Period of history
57. - up, excited
58. Concentric
64. Line about which a rotation occurs
66. Bustle or fuss (Colloq) (2-2)
67. Mediterranean country
68. Temple
69. Goes to law
70. One of the Leeward Islands
71. Verge
72. Formerly
73. Eminent

DOWN
1. Venture
2. Encourage in wrongdoing
3. Snack
4. Most parched
5. Rare metallic element
6. Infatuated
7. Gemstone
8. Savoury jelly
9. Abate
10. Gardening tool
11. Dug-in
12. Fragrant oil
13. Poetry
21. Torpedo vessel (1-4)
22. Enough
26. Set of clothing
27. Labels
28. Double curve
29. Banishing
30. Military detachment
31. Indian guitar-like instrument
35. Concern
37. Hollow in the earth
38. Overwhelmed
40. Mast
42. Monetary unit of Zambia
45. Hindu sect
47. Working for
50. Fourth highest peak in the world
52. Rat-catching animal
53. Abrade
54. Group of six
55. Love affair
59. Lyric poems
60. Expense
61. Rant
62. Hip bones
63. Vesicle
65. Perceive with the eyes

Puzzle 93

ACROSS
1. Surmise
6. Remain
10. Nervous
14. Grain fungus
15. Indian exercise method
16. Of thou
17. Aggression (Colloq)
18. Ark builder
19. Scene of first miracle
20. A limit
23. Vase
24. Consume
25. Types of pasta
27. Club
32. Chapter of the Koran
33. Grain beard
34. Surround
36. Long stories
39. Metal
41. Signet
43. Beak
44. Purple
46. Hungarian wine
48. Fish eggs
49. Seaward
51. Cured
53. Mexican-American girl
56. Prefix, before
57. Norse goddess
58. Take apart
64. Hip bones
66. Dairy product
67. Pertaining to the palm of the hand
68. Linelike
69. Relax
70. Decorate
71. Booth
72. Frozen precipitation
73. Narrow body parts

DOWN
1. Cog
2. Exhort
3. Ova
4. Graded
5. Charge for storing goods
6. Synchronize
7. Trumpet sound
8. Encore
9. Louts
10. Etcetera
11. A peak of the Himalayas
12. Genus
13. Lambs
21. Units
22. Intellect
26. Dull
27. Sphere
28. Monetary unit of Angola
29. Futile
30. Funeral notice
31. African antelope
35. Argument
37. Drug-yielding plant
38. Toboggan
40. Flat circular plate
42. Lanterns
45. No longer living
47. Capital of Armenia
50. Resins
52. Make old fashioned
53. Freeze
54. Prefix, sun
55. Indian or Chinese
59. Too
60. Oblique
61. Political combine
62. Songbird
63. Sea eagles
65. Affirmative vote

Puzzle 94

ACROSS
1. Levels
6. Sovereign
10. Nocturnal birds
14. Accustom
15. Ethereal
16. Lash
17. Roofer
18. Pant
19. One of Columbus's ships
20. Explaining clearly
23. Cardinal number
24. Greek letter
25. Brazes
27. Surpass
32. Liquid food
33. Wildebeest
34. Celts and Gaels
36. Brag
39. Italian currency
41. Chronicle
43. Desex female dog
44. Alcohol burners
46. Spanish river
48. Go wrong
49. Ardent
51. Libertine
53. Situated near the kidneys
56. Organ of hearing
57. Pair
58. Chimneys
64. Adjoin
66. Once again
67. Choice steak (1-4)
68. Glass panel
69. Basic unit of heredity
70. Arm joint
71. Ocean fluctuation
72. Greek god of love
73. Relaxes

DOWN
1. Ritual
2. Indigo
3. Bantu tribesman
4. Builds
5. Arranged in series
6. Narrative of heroic exploits
7. Warmth
8. Upbeat
9. Greek god of sleep
10. Possess
11. Official government report
12. Passenger vessel
13. Extends across
21. Indian millet
22. Soft roundish lump
26. Twosomes
27. Look at amorously
28. Single entity
29. Reversal in circumstances
30. Is not
31. Pertaining to punishment
35. Palm starch
37. Hindu garment
38. Novice
40. Roof overhang
42. Stringed instruments
45. Transgressions
47. Break into many pieces
50. Harm
52. Fit for tillage
53. Change to suit
54. One of the United Arab Emirates
55. One who dislikes company
59. Game of chance
60. Female sheep
61. Male swans
62. Gnarl
63. Stitches
65. Golf peg

Puzzle 95

ACROSS
1. More certain
6. Monkeys
10. Pinnacle
14. Express opinions
15. Martial art
16. Hoodwink
17. Loses heat
18. Sour
19. Indian currency
20. Preventing fever
23. Male cat
24. Ocean
25. Wave riders
27. Roofed with straw
32. Unstable lepton
33. Long period of time
34. The Pentateuch
36. Hindu scripture
39. Top
41. Monsters
43. Person who lies
44. Citrus fruits
46. Fits of rage
48. Monad
49. Minerals
51. Formerly Ceylon
53. Social worker in a hospital
56. Gist
57. Change colour of
58. In accordance with tradition
64. Prefix, eight
66. Soon
67. Hag
68. Make beer
69. Unskilled laborer
70. Consumed
71. Nobleman
72. Garment edges
73. Swings to the side

DOWN
1. Caribbean dance music
2. Atop
3. Uproar
4. Sign up
5. Esteem
6. Partly open
7. Brownish purple
8. Redacts
9. - chloride, common salt
10. Exclamation of surprise
11. Dispute
12. Feudal estate
13. Tests
21. Lout
22. Shank
26. Disgusting
27. Freshwater duck
28. American Indian
29. Wind speed measuring instrument
30. Work units
31. Mends socks
35. Scion
37. Tier
38. Region
40. Prefix, dry
42. Skimp
45. Dispatched
47. Water channels
50. Angel
52. Away from the mouth
53. Sun-dried brick
54. Elastic material
55. Indian princess
59. Fate
60. Taverns
61. Musical symbol
62. Once more
63. Optical device
65. Nocturnal bird

Puzzle 96

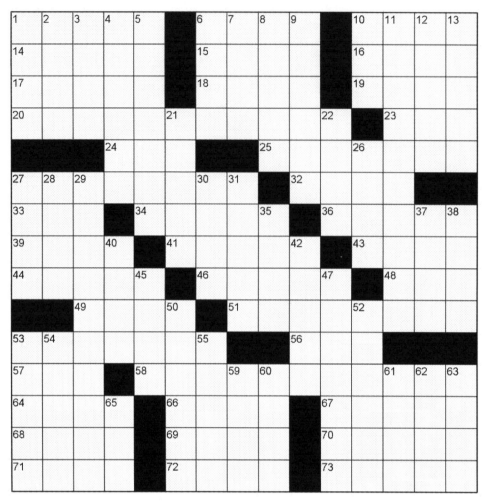

ACROSS
1. Loses colour
6. Travelled on
10. Beaten by tennis service
14. Resinous compound
15. Laughing sound (2.2)
16. Military body
17. Drive back
18. Epic poetry
19. Cut ruthlessly
20. Unifying
23. Scottish river
24. 21st letter of the Greek alphabet
25. Breathes in
27. Doublecrosser (3-5)
32. An auction
33. Electrical resistance unit
34. - and credit
36. Ski course
39. Male offspring
41. Swiss song
43. Having a toe
44. Greets
46. Link
48. Annoy by persistent faultfinding
49. Whimper
51. Irregular
53. Odorous substance
56. Former measure of length
57. Mine
58. Ancient
64. Wood choppers
66. Metallic element
67. Conscious
68. Floor covering
69. Crocodile (Colloq)
70. Narrow joining pieces
71. Third son of Adam
72. Obsolete form of has
73. Rendezvous

DOWN
1. Comrade
2. Primates
3. Drugs
4. Free from
5. Young sylph
6. Ostrichlike bird
7. Expression used when accident happens
8. Loincloth worn by Hindu men
9. Red dyes
10. Exclamation of surprise
11. Lullaby
12. Master of ceremonies
13. Levees
21. British sailor
22. A bloke
26. Got down from mount
27. Nonsense
28. Command to horse
29. Infinite in power
30. Black
31. Travels on
35. Passage of Bible
37. Freshwater duck
38. Nervously irritable
40. Elide
42. Baits
45. Smack
47. Leaping
50. Enhance
52. Look of anger
53. Iridescent gems
54. Large iron camp-oven
55. The Earth
59. Loud derisory cry
60. Unit of length
61. Suggestive
62. Annoys
63. Girdle
65. Scale note

Puzzle 97

ACROSS
1. Loose outer garment
6. Small yeast cake
10. Incite
14. Ski cabin
15. Consumer
16. Hammer head
17. Mimicry
18. Rhythmic swing
19. Native of Scotland
20. Removed governmental restraints from
23. Poem
24. Sin
25. More slender
27. Salable
32. Break suddenly
33. Period of human life
34. Song of praise
36. Genuflect
39. Naive person
41. Pertaining to birth
43. To
44. Bordered
46. Abnormal body temperature
48. Former coin of France
49. Medicinal plant
51. Fragrant
53. Strollers
56. Tibetan gazelle
57. Zodiac sign
58. Withered stalk of grass
64. Mountain lake
66. Ripped
67. Coronet
68. Merely
69. Submachine gun
70. Gravel ridge
71. River of Hades
72. Russian no
73. Ostrich-like birds

DOWN
1. Dressed
2. Bound
3. River in central Europe
4. Concurred
5. Chief stagehand
6. Papal edict
7. Largest continent
8. Leather straps
9. Russian cooperatives
10. Raises
11. Remunerate
12. Rock cavity
13. Go in
21. Metropolitan
22. Double on a bicycle (Colloq)
26. Hindu lawgiver
27. Weathercock
28. Minor oath
29. Friendly
30. Foliage unit
31. Something that consumes
35. Wheel hub
37. English college
38. Yahoo
40. Sense
42. Flat shelf
45. Sketched
47. Cock
50. Native of Britain
52. Somewhat overdue
53. Singers
54. Intended
55. White-haired
59. Endure
60. Pre Easter season
61. Agricultural implement
62. Extent of space
63. Battles
65. Greek goddess of night

Puzzle 98

ACROSS
1. Father
6. Gull-like predatory bird
10. Vomit
14. Dwelling
15. Bits of thread
16. Bone of the forearm
17. Russian revolutionary leader
18. Military detachment
19. Cat
20. Voting districts
23. Young dog
24. Gratuity
25. Meal courses
27. Root vegetables
32. Antlered beast
33. Chop
34. Cunning
36. A Welshman (Colloq)
39. Untidy person
41. Butcher's wares
43. Delete (Printing)
44. Chinese
46. The aforesaid
48. Bovine
49. Wildebeest
51. Newborn infants
53. Word formed by transposing letters of another
56. Vigor
57. Cheat
58. Bright ideas
64. Facial feature
66. Migrant farm worker
67. Stupid person
68. Flower
69. Salamander
70. Large ray
71. Impressed
72. Gravel
73. Senior

DOWN
1. Wan
2. Cain's victim
3. Accent
4. Decrees
5. Hiring
6. Insult
7. Basic currency of Papua New Guinea
8. Join
9. Be present at
10. Have supper
11. More than perfect
12. Follow
13. Hornets
21. Drug obtained from poppies
22. Printer's mark, keep
26. Peruse
27. Move past
28. Wheel shaft
29. Redeploy
30. Particoloured
31. Killed
35. Suffix, diminutive
37. Floating ice
38. Evergreen trees
40. Singer, - Crosby
42. Halts
45. Restrain
47. Former (3-4)
50. Malay garment
52. Footless
53. Capital of Ghana
54. In no way at all
55. Creator
59. Hawaiian honeycreeper
60. After deductions
61. Skin
62. Dust speck
63. Leading player
65. - Kelly

Puzzle 99

ACROSS
1. Implied
6. Polluted atmosphere
10. Exclamation of mild dismay
14. Form of oxygen
15. Coffin cover
16. Hungarian sheepdog
17. Mediterranean island
18. Assistant
19. Submachine gun
20. Situated within the heart
23. Purse
24. Egg drink
25. Originate
27. Cabbage salad
32. Dirt
33. Reverential fear
34. Practitioners of yoga
36. Parboil
39. Clothes-pins
41. Inflict (vengeance)
43. Leg joint
44. Prepares for publication
46. Sacrificial bench
48. Metal container
49. Fine powder
51. Person swearing to statement
53. Helices
56. "The Raven" author
57. Sew
58. Contests
64. Dutch cheese
66. American Indian
67. Perfect
68. Overdue
69. Japanese syllabic script
70. Run off
71. Went by plane
72. Store
73. Modernise

DOWN
1. Heavy book
2. Islamic call to prayer
3. Chill
4. Chant
5. Covering to keep a teapot hot (3-4)
6. Stout pole
7. Female servant
8. A parent
9. Twinkles
10. Operations (colloq)
11. Outweigh
12. Garment tuck
13. Scorch
21. Glowing
22. South-east Asian nation
26. Notch
27. Cloak
28. Was indebted
29. Lawful
30. Taj Mahal site
31. Brandish
35. Surfeit
37. Thin
38. Depression in a surface
40. Celestial body
42. Tenth letter of the Greek alphabet
45. Lath
47. More spacious
50. Timepieces
52. Sewing requisite
53. Ledge
54. Foot lever
55. Twilled fabric of silk
59. U.S. divorce city
60. Tides that attain the least height
61. Lighting gas
62. Record conversation
63. Swing to the side
65. Cat's sound

Puzzle 100

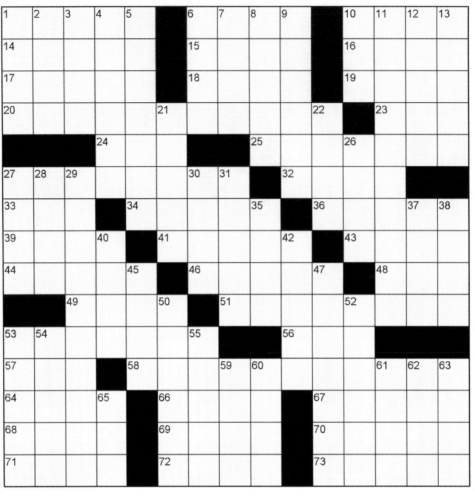

ACROSS
1. Strike
6. South American Indian
10. Roman dates
14. Brother of Moses
15. Chief god of ancient Greece
16. This thing
17. Lord
18. Prohibits
19. Wise
20. Something converted from one language to another
23. Last month
24. Fire remains
25. Prophets
27. Stop
32. The Pentateuch
33. Wrath
34. Russian emperors
36. Cane product
39. Speech impediment
41. Bide one's time
43. Bulk
44. Large body of water
46. Gape
48. Decay
49. Person who lies
51. Omitting
53. Severe mental retardation
56. 7th letter of the Greek alphabet
57. Resinous deposit
58. Without offense
64. Rectangular pier
66. Public swimming pool
67. The cream
68. Monetary unit of Cambodia
69. Greek goddess of strife
70. Idiot
71. Compelled
72. Third son of Adam
73. Broomed

DOWN
1. - Disney
2. Tress
3. Region
4. French brandy
5. Parliament of Israel
6. Log house of rural Russia
7. Tidy
8. Object d'art
9. Classify
10. Sexless things
11. A peak of the Himalayas
12. Bird of prey
13. Cancels a deletion
21. Capital of Tibet
22. Temple
26. Shank
27. Structure for storing grain
28. Of urine
29. Re-chose
30. Carpentry tools
31. Muse of poetry
35. Thailand
37. Northern arm of the Black Sea
38. Network of nerves
40. Ache
42. Attempts
45. Western pact
47. Reveres
50. Ransacks
52. Wan
53. Cause panic
54. A craze
55. On fire
59. Prepare for publication
60. Food
61. Ireland
62. Halt
63. Dispatched
65. Beer

Puzzle 101

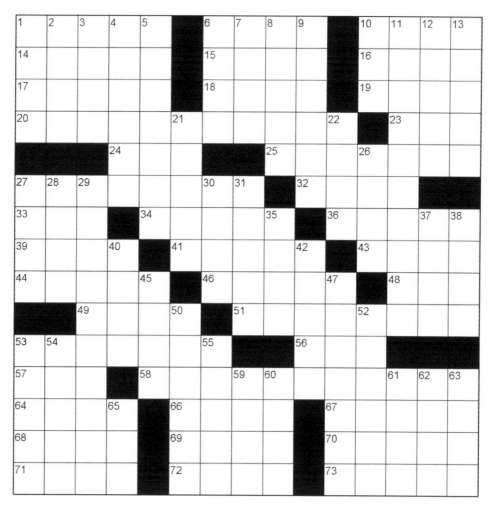

ACROSS
1. Rush
6. Informed
10. Mop
14. Epileptic seizure
15. Nautical call
16. 11th letter of the Hebrew alphabet
17. Long lock of hair
18. Capital of Shaanxi province, China
19. Largest continent
20. Dramatic
23. A dynasty in China
24. Soap ingredient
25. Grinning
27. Fitted new back parts to shoes
32. Portent
33. Wood sorrel
34. Demon
36. African
39. Lash
41. Gaseous element
43. Breeding horse
44. Leather strip
46. Indian princess
48. Monad
49. Agitate
51. Paints again
53. Volatile petroleum distillate
56. Part of a circle
57. Atmosphere
58. Aglet
64. Manger
66. Sleeps briefly
67. City in Nebraska
68. U.S. divorce city
69. Shakespeare's river
70. Cooks in oven
71. Nervous
72. Time of abstinence
73. Foe

DOWN
1. Strikes
2. Land measure
3. Submachine gun
4. Struggle
5. Tried
6. Cab
7. U.S. State
8. Borrowings
9. Generator
10. Jamaican popular music
11. First U.S. president
12. Of bees
13. Cannabis
21. Early form of FAX
22. Delineate
26. Dreg
27. Arguments
28. Authentic
29. Spring used for timepiece
30. At any time
31. Arabian currency
35. Solitary
37. Small animal
38. Poems
40. Walkway
42. Asian country
45. Middle Eastern bread
47. Lower part of the external ear
50. Nasal
52. Person who delivers ice
53. Mother-of-pearl
54. Ventilated
55. Aloe
59. On top of
60. Is not
61. Grasp
62. Those
63. Simple
65. Lad

Puzzle 102

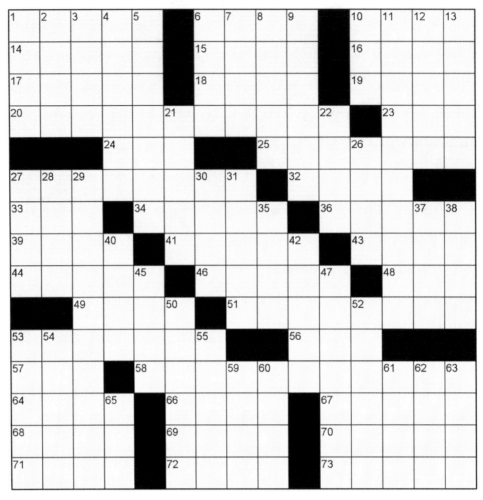

ACROSS
1. Baron
6. Basis
10. Ebony
14. Lustrous black
15. In bed
16. Public swimming pool
17. Loudly
18. French military cap
19. Nourishment
20. Having dentils
23. Owing
24. Evening
25. Chiefs
27. Sacrosanctly
32. Lees
33. Expression of disgust
34. South Korea's capital
36. Anorak
39. Foss
41. Brown and white Eurasian falcon
43. Come to ground
44. Leers
46. Small pit
48. Carried out
49. Secular
51. Beautiful young maidens
53. Sleeping sickness flies
56. Monkey
57. Flee
58. Unbridled
64. Exhort
66. Unspecified in number
67. Monastery of an abbot
68. Killed
69. Exclude
70. Cavalry sword
71. Wheel cover
72. Charge per unit
73. African antelope

DOWN
1. Type of jazz
2. Robust
3. River in central England
4. Asexual
5. Salad herbs
6. Capital of Azerbaijan
7. Second son of Adam and Eve
8. Flower part
9. Redacted
10. Fairy
11. Break down into harmless products
12. Smell
13. Knobs
21. Yields
22. Wyatt -
26. Distribute cards
27. Form of wrestling
28. Eager
29. U.S. space shuttle
30. To be idle
31. Canadian province
35. Tax
37. Grow together
38. Increases
40. Nipple
42. Rechart
45. Spanish words of agreement (2.2)
47. Placate
50. Government morals protector
52. Consisting of herbs
53. Faith
54. Bad-tempered
55. Mouthlike opening
59. Send out
60. Measure out
61. Swedish pop-group of the '70s
62. Sea bird
63. Having eyes
65. Female sheep

Puzzle 103

ACROSS
1. Sulky
6. A bloke
10. Offscourings
14. Wading bird
15. Vow
16. Cabbagelike plant
17. Vigilant
18. Towards the centre
19. Ancient Peruvian
20. Altering
23. Seine
24. Lubricant
25. Coals
27. Unselfish concern
32. Hood-like membrane
33. Automobile
34. Creator
36. Breathed rattlingly
39. Officiating priest of a mosque
41. Malay martial art
43. Cupola
44. Pythias's friend
46. Wigwam
48. A fool
49. High roll of hair
51. Infinite time
53. Dental
56. Actress, - West
57. The sun
58. Self-confident
64. Cut
66. Peruse
67. Hives
68. Adolescent pimples
69. Comic person
70. Scope
71. Marsh plant
72. Greek god of love
73. Church official

DOWN
1. Pome
2. Leer
3. Fertiliser
4. Great fear
5. Rare metallic element
6. Piece of money
7. Drape
8. Loft
9. Of speech sounds
10. Snow runner
11. Tubular pasta
12. Peptic complaint
13. Butcher's wares
21. Assumed name
22. Growl
26. Couple
27. Etching fluid
28. Tibetan monk
29. Jumping apparatus used by acrobats
30. Short parody
31. Skirmish
35. Engrossed
37. Send out
38. Refuse
40. Luna
42. Abounds
45. Crazy (Colloq)
47. Deletion
50. Violent in force
52. Of nerves
53. Academy Award
54. Soft
55. Distinct
59. Gambling game
60. Appends
61. Tear
62. Verge
63. Performer
65. Prefix, foot

Puzzle 104

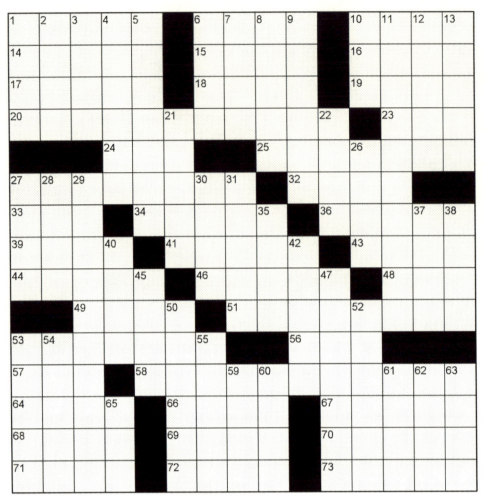

ACROSS
1. Ante
6. Pedal digits
10. Eh?
14. Of Nordic stock
15. Italian capital
16. Vow
17. Monetary unit of Nigeria
18. Northern arm of the Black Sea
19. Solely
20. Instrument for measuring mechanical force
23. Weir
24. Unit of weight
25. Give sexual feelings to
27. Coffeecake topping
32. Narcotics agent
33. Reverential fear
34. Sum up
36. Ethic
39. Bites
41. Chinese secret society
43. Valley
44. Biting insects
46. Incites
48. Enemy
49. Hoot
51. Tailor
53. Exceed
56. Ignited
57. Japanese sash
58. Rebuild
64. Ark builder
66. Drink to excess
67. Athlete's foot
68. Fence opening
69. Goes to law
70. Sins
71. Type of gun
72. Sea eagles
73. Brings home

DOWN
1. Beach feature
2. Salver
3. 16th letter of the Hebrew alphabet
4. Self-defense
5. Endear
6. Streetcar
7. Seep
8. Affect emotion
9. Welsh river
10. Court
11. Manual skill
12. Collection of maps
13. Seasoning herb
21. Beginning
22. Wander
26. Walked
27. Carolled
28. One of two identical people
29. Return to native land
30. Colour of unbleached linen
31. Dens
35. Leaf of a book
37. Agave
38. Ogle
40. Cease
42. Trade agreements
45. Fly high
47. Struck
50. Sleeping sickness fly
52. Work hard for
53. Carols
54. German submarine
55. Purge
59. Candid
60. Promontory
61. Single entity
62. Gael
63. Soviet news service
65. Female bird

Puzzle 105

ACROSS
1. Brink
6. At sea
10. Suspicious (Colloq)
14. Person born under the sign of the Ram
15. Waist band
16. Upon
17. Lasso
18. Boss on a shield
19. Charge over property
20. Calculations
23. Craze
24. Fish appendage
25. Greet
27. American Indian
32. Small valley
33. Money (Slang)
34. Goatlike antelope
36. Flower
39. 27th president of the U.S
41. Grassy plain
43. Father
44. Went wrong
46. Dropsy
48. Faucet
49. Responsibility
51. Struts
53. Four-wheeled carriages
56. That woman
57. Fitting
58. Reduced involvement in (hostilities)
64. Golf mounds
66. June 6, 1944
67. Avoid
68. Fleet rodent
69. Ova
70. Twill-weave fabric
71. Inner Hebrides island
72. Chair
73. Deride

DOWN
1. Turbine blade
2. Greek god of love
3. Public disturbance
4. Convert into a gas
5. Foes
6. Adjoin
7. Prefix, part
8. Arm joint
9. Made amends
10. The sun
11. Having only one leaf
12. Water vapour
13. Atmospheric probe
21. Chronicle
22. Sledge
26. Applaud
27. Pigeon coop
28. Rime
29. Barefaced audacity
30. Egypt's river
31. Minor oath
35. Once again
37. Stout pole
38. Yelps
40. Propend
42. City in Nebraska
45. Couple
47. Eternal
50. Soft leathers
52. Carved (image)
53. Slats
54. More or less vertical
55. Rush-like plant
59. Heroic story
60. Wen
61. Weight allowance
62. Brink
63. Animal
65. Witness

Puzzle 106

ACROSS
1. Injures
6. Envelop
10. Blue shade
14. - Heep, Dickens character
15. River in central Switzerland
16. Bindi-eye prickle
17. Pass into disuse
18. Church recess
19. Bird prison
20. Pertaining to an abstract
23. New Zealand parrot
24. Wane
25. Hunting dogs
27. Resembling glass
32. Hamlet
33. Anger
34. Tinged
36. Standards
39. Competes
41. Italian monies
43. Fate
44. Flower
46. Steals
48. Yoko -
49. Dutch name of The Hague
51. Quibble over trifles
53. Haunt
56. Vase
57. Biblical high priest
58. Scattering
64. Uncivil
66. Fitted with shoes
67. Water wheel
68. Energy units
69. Robust
70. Concede
71. Fat
72. Seaward
73. Alcohol burners

DOWN
1. Hawaiian dance
2. Semite
3. Tears
4. Boss
5. Fruit-flavored ice
6. Member of the women's army auxiliary corps
7. Ecstatic
8. Upbeat
9. Annoyed
10. Government broadcaster
11. Built to withstand an earthquake
12. Tout
13. Regions
21. Boiling
22. English college
26. Stepped
27. Exclamation of acclaim
28. Eye part
29. Alveolar ridge
30. Single entity
31. Remnant
35. Steal
37. Prefix, one
38. Polluted atmosphere
40. Marine mammal
42. Organization
45. Incursion
47. Peculiar
50. Japanese dancing girl
52. Twist inward
53. Fathers
54. Ayers Rock
55. Vedic deity
59. Foot part
60. Notion
61. Republic in SW Asia
62. One of Columbus's ships
63. Guns (Slang)
65. Superlative suffix

Puzzle 107

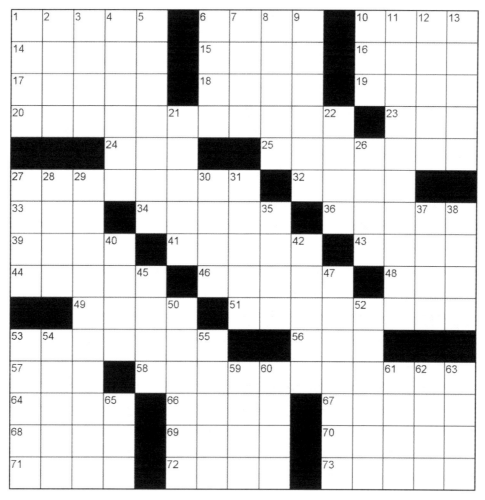

ACROSS
1. Gourd
6. Circular course
10. Shoo
14. White poplar tree
15. Sly look
16. Step
17. Copy with stencils
18. Relaxation
19. Pain
20. Putting at risk
23. - up, excited
24. 19th letter of the Greek alphabet
25. Foster or promote
27. Sugar apple
32. Farm wagon
33. Female fowl
34. Alcohol burners
36. Composition for nine
39. Profane expression
41. Group of eight
43. Cab
44. Trinity
46. Applause
48. Decade
49. Hint
51. Cut into two equal parts
53. Good for nothing
56. Etcetera
57. Edge
58. A short distance (6,5)
64. Once more
66. From a distance
67. Run away with a lover
68. Alley
69. Hints
70. Revolt
71. Location
72. The Orient
73. Outlay

DOWN
1. Female horse
2. Black
3. Advance money
4. Salt of oleic acid
5. Newborn infant
6. Exultation
7. 365 days
8. Gum
9. Before this
10. Mineral spring
11. Laugh loudly
12. Pains
13. Fangs
21. Zest
22. South American bird
26. Uproar
27. Fired a gun
28. Erode
29. Lure
30. A single time
31. Mend garments
35. Bargain event
37. Executive Officer
38. Hue
40. Meeting centre
42. Lady knights
45. Membership fees
47. Giggles
50. Worldly goods
52. Carry with great effort
53. European mountains
54. Mountain where Moses received the law
55. Bulgaria's capital
59. Sleeps briefly
60. Former
61. Gown
62. Candid
63. Fuse together
65. Tiny

Puzzle 108

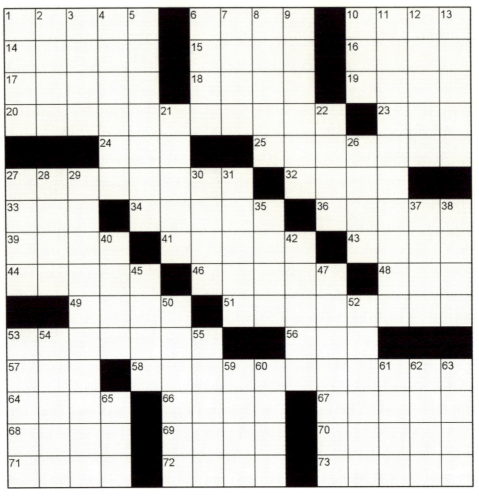

ACROSS
1. Stale smelling
6. Girl
10. Aggregate
14. Cave
15. Military force
16. Continuous dull pain
17. Iron product
18. Unskilled laborer
19. Inert gaseous element
20. Apparatus for recording bets
23. Passenger vehicle
24. Former weight for wool
25. Teach
27. Occurring throughout a city
32. - Connery
33. An age
34. Regretful
36. Dandies
39. College residential building
41. Microwave emitter
43. Scandinavian
44. Contribution to discussion
46. Outfit
48. Tibetan gazelle
49. Highly excited
51. Most inane
53. Group of stars
56. Even (poet.)
57. Norse goddess
58. Explaining clearly
64. Eager
66. Soon
67. Spanish Mister
68. City in W Nevada
69. Cattle parasite
70. Assume
71. Network
72. Gooey (Colloq)
73. Full of stones

DOWN
1. Spar
2. To
3. Let it stand
4. Formal agreement
5. Takes on jaundiced appearance
6. Drinks (as a cat)
7. Extent of space
8. Struck
9. Church councils
10. Adult male
11. Elasticized bandage
12. Cry out loudly
13. Sanity
21. Expression peculiar to a language
22. Regretted
26. Hood-like membrane
27. Basic monetary unit of Ghana
28. Press clothes
29. Canvas coverings
30. Haul
31. Celts and Gaels
35. Abominable snowman
37. Epic poetry
38. Petty quarrel
40. Drinking vessels
42. Reigned
45. Carry
47. Gratifies
50. Ice cream made with eggs
52. Eager
53. Bewitch
54. Embankment
55. Mysterious
59. Rooster
60. Resembling ink
61. Prefix, India
62. Part of speech
63. Dull colour
65. Scale note

Puzzle 109

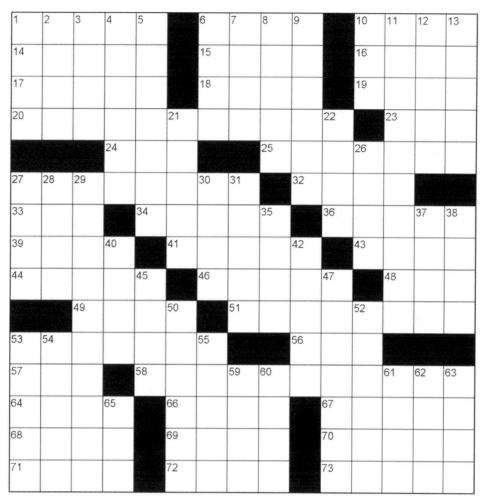

ACROSS
1. Without humour
6. Surface to air missiles
10. At sea
14. Weird
15. Indigo
16. Benedictine monks' titles
17. Ink stains
18. Left
19. Draw by suction
20. Occurring at the same time
23. Born
24. Hasten
25. Bossed
27. Conveys
32. Pile
33. Black bird
34. Skilled
36. Soiled
39. Pair of oxen
41. Grain stores
43. Just passable (2-2)
44. Type of turnip
46. Nest
48. Large tree
49. Blackbird
51. Back and forth movement (2.3.3)
53. Carrier (of news)
56. Victory sign
57. Actor, - Chaney
58. Overconfident
64. Chances
66. Agave
67. More uncivil
68. High-pitched tone
69. East Indies palm
70. Dropsy
71. Alkali
72. Adolescent
73. Devil

DOWN
1. Debutantes
2. Depend
3. Press clothes
4. Chinese fruit
5. Orthodox Jewish school
6. Palm starch
7. Soon
8. Son of Zeus
9. Detective
10. Commercials
11. Impervious to sound
12. Master of ceremonies
13. Inquired
21. Marsh plants
22. Took legal action against
26. Speaking platform
27. Parts of week
28. Enough
29. Having a similar opinion
30. Riding strap
31. Rive
35. Bustle or fuss (Colloq) (2-2)
37. Russian emperor
38. - Ono
40. Paradise
42. Debonair
45. Therefore
47. Derided
50. East Mediterrranean region
52. Strip
53. Jelly-like masses
54. Cowboy exhibition
55. Tell an untruth again
59. Thick cord
60. Train away from
61. As previously given
62. Verne's submariner
63. Grandmother
65. Mineral spring

Puzzle 110

ACROSS
1. Feet coverings
6. Hew
10. Pole
14. Concur
15. First-class
16. Mysterious symbol
17. Investigation
18. Whirl
19. English public school
20. Estrangements
23. Auction item
24. Plead
25. Nut confections
27. Cutting instrument for paper
32. Lighting gas
33. Electrically charged atom
34. Move stealthily
36. Extinct birds
39. Lets head fall wearily
41. W.A. eucalypts
43. Dossier
44. Heroic tales
46. Judges
48. Transgress
49. Soft drink variety
51. Photograph
53. Great speakers
56. Acne pimple
57. Cavity
58. Violent fight
64. Ardent
66. Pen
67. Sun-dried brick
68. Molten rock
69. Hip bones
70. Monetary unit of Zambia
71. Swing to the side
72. Lump of clay
73. Informs

DOWN
1. Undermines
2. Monster
3. Harvest
4. Skewered meat portions
5. Prophetess
6. Fling
7. American Indian
8. Pungent bulb
9. Pennant
10. Prefix, before
11. Having a foreign appearance
12. Snub
13. Camp shelters
21. Severe pain
22. Took legal action against
26. Blunder
27. Trigonometric function
28. Fowl enclosure
29. Suggestive
30. Peruse
31. Cloys
35. Sharp
37. Potpourri
38. Dispatched
40. Native of Scotland
42. Mixture of smoke and haze
45. Slovenly person
47. Fricative
50. Semitic language
52. Gorge
53. Iridescent gems
54. Emulate
55. Motionless
59. Group of three persons
60. Burden
61. Howl
62. Cain's victim
63. Dreg
65. Black bird

Puzzle 111

ACROSS
1. A loom attachment
6. Glide on surface
10. Chooses
14. Toward the port side
15. Attention
16. Very dry champagne
17. Rekindled
18. Got down from mount
19. Alkali
20. Ventures
23. Sailor
24. Evergreen tree
25. Containers
27. Pursuant
32. Shower
33. Monad
34. Money
36. Light refractor
39. Immerses
41. Stir
43. Suffix, diminutive
44. Olios
46. Boat spines
48. Of us
49. Polynesian carved image
51. Semisweet white wine
53. Roots
56. Level of karate proficiency
57. Flying mammal
58. Having God as the focal point
64. Funeral notice
66. Askew
67. Daughter of one's brother or sister
68. Overhanging lower edge of a roof
69. Allows
70. More gelid
71. Submachine gun
72. Formerly
73. Perfume with incense

DOWN
1. Venture
2. Candid
3. Threaded fastener
4. Underpants
5. Rare metallic element
6. Mark left by a healed wound
7. Wife of Shiva
8. Erse
9. Space rock
10. Observation
11. Precursor
12. Royal house
13. Plunges knife into
21. Earlier
22. Hit with hand
26. Dreadful
27. Seed containers
28. Single entity
29. Reiterant
30. Cosy corner
31. Pastes
35. Seaward
37. Astound
38. Lake or pond
40. Drink greedily
42. Evade
45. Short parody
47. Containing tin
50. Breathe in
52. Lure
53. Hautboys
54. Capital of Morocco
55. Waste drain
59. Food scraps
60. Vesicle
61. Riding strap
62. Frozen confections
63. Cover with wax
65. Cardinal number

Puzzle 112

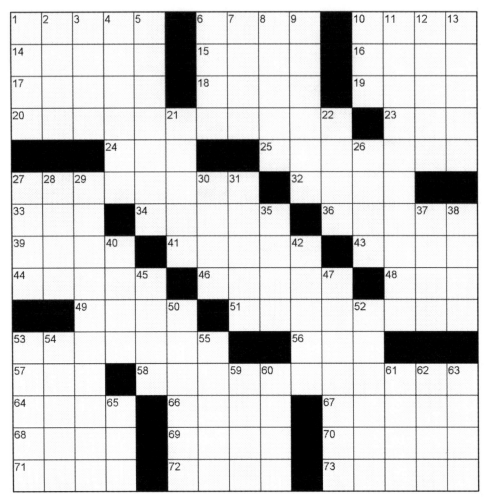

ACROSS
1. Rich tapestry
6. - Lisa
10. Italian city
14. Leaven
15. Black
16. Little devils
17. In good time
18. Anon
19. Epic poetry
20. Somnambulist
23. Fish eggs
24. Greek letter
25. Small plates
27. Sanatorium
32. Dregs
33. Fitting
34. Prison rooms
36. Theatrical entertainment
39. Wife of Jacob
41. Consumed again
43. Crude minerals
44. Group of eight
46. Nematocyst
48. Writing fluid
49. Angers
51. Haughty
53. Mouth-like orifices
56. Before
57. Brown shade
58. Dissimilarities
64. Toward the mouth
66. Midday
67. Coral island
68. Skin opening
69. Walked
70. Abrupt
71. Eye inflammation
72. Hardens
73. Finished

DOWN
1. Affirmative votes
2. Genuine
3. Uncommon
4. Dormant
5. Astringent
6. Rocky tableland
7. Ancient Greek coin
8. Cosy corners
9. Fuse pottery or glass
10. Pastry item
11. Director
12. Trail of a wild animal
13. Donkeys
21. Aqua
22. Regretted
26. King mackerel
27. Nimbus
28. Oil cartel
29. Not moving
30. Smart - , show-off
31. Grassy plain
35. Agitate
37. List of dishes
38. Questions
40. Injure
42. Grass trimming tool
45. Deceased
47. Gilded
50. Skimps
52. Suitable for Lent
53. Halts
54. Fortune-telling cards
55. Before
59. Animal's paw
60. Finishes
61. Thin rope
62. Otherwise
63. Toboggan
65. Scottish river

Puzzle 113

ACROSS
1. Forded
6. Gust
10. Performs
14. Think
15. Reside
16. Shirt
17. Item having exchange value
18. Augury
19. Leg joint
20. Music, gradually decreasing in loudness
23. Henpeck
24. Oxlike African antelope
25. Groups of seven
27. The words of an infant
32. Grudge fight
33. Exploit
34. Equalises
36. Bargain events
39. Falsehoods
41. Make law
43. Monetary unit of Nigeria
44. Reveals
46. Old wound marks
48. Not (prefix)
49. Guns (Slang)
51. Ravelling
53. Agile goat antelope
56. In favor of
57. Lever for rowing
58. Having good intentions
64. Helper
66. Greek goddess of the earth
67. Pale green mosslike lichen
68. Slanting
69. Days before
70. Sieves
71. Harmony
72. Third son of Adam
73. Laziness

DOWN
1. Blue dye plant
2. Church recess
3. Circular plate
4. Zest
5. A relaxing of international tension
6. Cartel
7. Citrus fruit
8. Kilns
9. Directed one's way
10. Question
11. Tubular pasta
12. Something special
13. Surfboard fins
21. Debonair
22. Musical work
26. Timber tree
27. Incandescent lamp
28. Largest continent
29. Outdoor tavern
30. Telescope part
31. Skill
35. Peruse
37. Black
38. A carol
40. A join
42. Literary device
45. Pack away
47. Austrian composer
50. Blockades
52. Throat part
53. Shore
54. Japanese poem
55. Bond servant
59. English court
60. Pulp
61. Information
62. After deductions
63. Wide slash
65. Female sheep

Puzzle 114

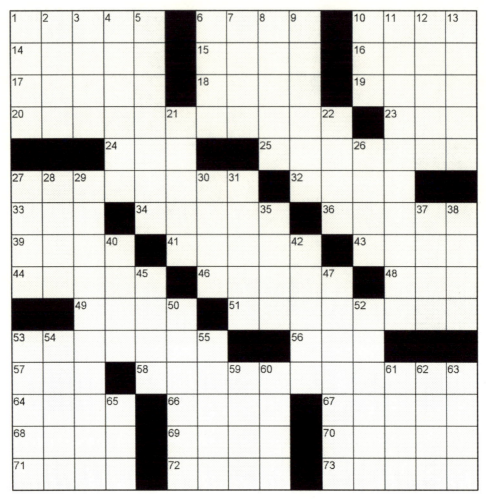

ACROSS
1. Prickly pear
6. Royal House
10. Prefix, eight
14. African antelope
15. One who is indebted
16. Large mollusc
17. Slews
18. Hereditary factor
19. Stimulate
20. Kill
23. Racket
24. Doctor
25. Chiefs
27. Japanese scroll
32. Malay dagger with a wavy blade
33. Affirmative vote
34. Choose
36. Foot-operated lever
39. English county
41. Is foolishly fond of
43. Savoury Mexican dish
44. Analyze a metalic compound
46. Narrow body parts
48. Monetary unit of Romania
49. Egyptian deity
51. Leanest
53. Cooked with water vapour
56. The Lion
57. Killer whale
58. Gossip
64. Large trees
66. New Guinea currency unit
67. City in N central Nigeria
68. Prefix, thousand
69. Officiating priest of a mosque
70. Church official
71. Killed
72. Half burnt coal
73. Elides

DOWN
1. Exploding star
2. Crude minerals
3. Pastry items
4. Scrape
5. Supple
6. Practitioner of yoga
7. Submachine gun
8. Pertaining to the kidneys
9. Indonesian cigarette
10. Scottish expression
11. Breed of draft horse
12. Pig-like animal
13. Portents
21. Reprimand
22. Wyatt -
26. Daily fare of food
27. New Zealand parrot
28. Affirmative votes
29. Conspicuous
30. Inert gaseous element
31. Group of eight
35. Technician
37. Beats by tennis service
38. Oaf
40. Good-bye (2-2)
42. Talent
45. Edible roots
47. Exhales violently
50. Frenzied
52. Disallowed bowling delivery in cricket (2-4)
53. Cry-babies
54. Path
55. Cathedral
59. Furniture wood
60. Domesticate
61. Official language of Pakistan
62. Row
63. Sailors
65. Plant

Puzzle 115

ACROSS
1. Wood smoothing tool
6. Elide
10. Slightly open
14. Monetary unit of Saudi Arabia
15. Sharpen
16. Indifferent
17. Oily fruit
18. Eye part
19. African antelope
20. Instrument for measuring mechanical force
23. Manipulate
24. Pronoun
25. Enunciate
27. Capital of Malawi
32. Large marine food fish
33. Lyric poem
34. Late
36. Leans
39. Move along in a stream
41. African antelope
43. Weary
44. Representative
46. Danger
48. Sol
49. Distant
51. Vanquished
53. Celebrations
56. Cut off
57. Help
58. Measure of luminous intensity
64. Bard
66. Hindu garment
67. Brightly coloured lizard
68. As well as
69. Minerals
70. Set up again
71. Speech defect
72. Eft
73. Dints

DOWN
1. Goad
2. Bulb flower
3. 16th letter of the Hebrew alphabet
4. American Indian tribe
5. Earth, water, air, or fire
6. Spacing wedge
7. Tradition
8. Join
9. Dislike
10. Inquire of
11. Person who keeps a journal
12. Early form of sonar
13. Article of make-up
21. Keyboard instrument
22. Disorderly flight
26. Military detachment
27. Garret
28. Indolently
29. Female leopard
30. Enclose in paper
31. Bordered
35. Long ago
37. Genuine
38. Transmit
40. Float through air
42. Firearm
45. Secular
47. Spotted wild cat
50. Motive
52. Climax
53. Of a pontiff
54. Garlic-flavored mayonnaise
55. Trap
59. Sketched
60. Catalog
61. Give notice
62. Send out
63. Torn clothing
65. Apex

Puzzle 116

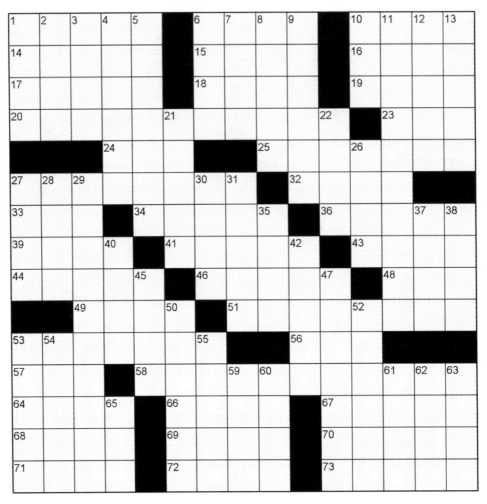

ACROSS
1. Enticed
6. Ravel
10. From a distance
14. Wear away
15. Capital of Italy
16. Sky color
17. Once more
18. Charity
19. Lively
20. Having dentils
23. Not good
24. Organ of hearing
25. Novelty
27. Loitering
32. Spool
33. North American nation
34. Descendant
36. Dish of raw vegetables
39. Of the highest quality
41. Ravine
43. Prince of India
44. Indian term of respect
46. Huge
48. Shoot a marble
49. Agave
51. Mosquitoes (Colloq)
53. Deer's horns
56. Period of history
57. Pastry item
58. Navy officer
64. Taj Mahal site
66. Bird's crop
67. Person used as one's excuse
68. Restraint
69. British National Gallery
70. Sicker
71. Type of jazz
72. Outbuilding
73. Greek letter

DOWN
1. Heavy metal
2. Incite
3. Brown and white horse
4. Prepared for publication
5. Refusals
6. German Mrs
7. Trundle
8. Capital of Jordan
9. Pertaining to yesterday
10. To endure
11. Fan-shaped
12. Subtle emanations
13. Marsh plants
21. Spasmodic cramp
22. Female sheep
26. Close to
27. Names
28. At sea
29. Launderette
30. African river
31. Hired thugs
35. Small recess
37. Partly open
38. Black birds
40. Up to the time of
42. Liberated
45. South African
47. Mythical ocean living female
50. Builds
52. Feudal tax
53. Away
54. African river
55. Mother of Isaac
59. Assess
60. Overwhelmed
61. Small rivulet
62. Encourage in wrongdoing
63. Monetary unit of Italy
65. Besides

Puzzle 117

ACROSS
1. Keyboard instrument
6. Spur
10. At the apex
14. Sprints
15. Arm bone
16. Upper respiratory tract infection
17. Excrete
18. Transgressions
19. Bird of prey
20. Choice cut of beef
23. The (German)
24. Card game
25. Tarries
27. Misled
32. Level
33. Handwoven Scandinavian rug
34. Prohibit
36. W.A. eucalypts
39. Vases
41. Parts played
43. Sloping walkway
44. Rears
46. Nidi
48. Bind
49. Nestling
51. Person who tends sheep
53. Cornmeal mush
56. Land measure
57. Petroleum
58. Implied meaning
64. Hit with hand
66. Scottish hills
67. Daring
68. Bristle
69. Restrain
70. Thigh and abdomen join
71. Paradise
72. Primordial giant in Norse myth
73. Atmospheric probe

DOWN
1. Prepare patient for operation
2. The villain in Othello
3. The maple
4. Snuggle
5. Bonelike
6. Spurt forth
7. Potpourri
8. Invalidate
9. Hyrax
10. Diving bird
11. Having three teeth
12. Marine mammal
13. Jetties
21. Wanderer
22. Jealousy
26. Cog
27. Thrash
28. Jaguarundi
29. Reticulate
30. Ebony
31. Valleys
35. 20th letter of the Hebrew alphabet
37. Islamic chieftain
38. Raced
40. Inner Hebrides island
42. Place
45. Without
47. Spas
50. Resembling a stub
52. Heterosexual (Colloq)
53. Body of deputised hunters
54. Lubricated
55. At right angles to a ships length
59. Against
60. Consumer
61. Metallic element
62. Roman poet
63. Hawaiian goose
65. Kitchen utensil

Puzzle 118

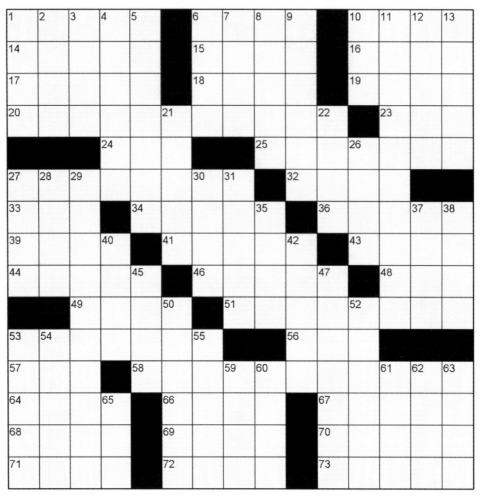

ACROSS
1. Organization
6. Headwear
10. Nocturnal birds
14. White poplar tree
15. Auricular
16. At what time
17. Baptismal vessels
18. Extra
19. Peruvian capital
20. That which one deserves
23. Drag
24. Honey
25. Traders
27. Prince of India
32. Crack
33. First woman
34. One who shapes metal
36. Slough
39. Bath requisite
41. Caper
43. Stout pole
44. Mountain range
46. Murders
48. Optic organ
49. South-east Asian nation
51. Empty language
53. Rident
56. Fish eggs
57. Move from side to side
58. U.S. marine
64. Authentic
66. Drug-yielding plant
67. A continuation (3-2)
68. Overdue
69. Retained
70. Fragrance
71. Be defeated
72. Broad ribbon
73. More modern

DOWN
1. Securely confined
2. Ebony
3. Portable shelter
4. Last syllable of a word
5. Harasses
6. Household
7. Small particle
8. Weary
9. Vistas
10. Nocturnal bird
11. Official government report
12. Madagascan mammal
13. Hitches
21. South American ruminant
22. Makes brown
26. Rules
27. Rocky tableland
28. Shakespeare's river
29. Motor vehicle lights
30. Quick jerky move
31. Loft
35. Small mountain
37. Yucatan indian
38. Prepare patient for operation
40. Resound
42. Irish county
45. Earth
47. Scotsman's pouch
50. Moves stealthily
52. Term of holding
53. Bulge
54. Portuguese territory in S China
55. Hood-shaped anatomical part
59. Outstanding
60. 8th letter of the Hebrew alphabet
61. Enough
62. Arrive
63. Knot in wood
65. Golfers mound

Puzzle 119

ACROSS
1. Temporary settlements
6. Australian trees
10. Relax
14. Ward off
15. Indigo
16. Avenues of escape
17. Giver
18. Floor covering
19. Printer's mark, keep
20. Counting
23. Single unit
24. Wages
25. Underwriter
27. Westernmost
32. Fat
33. Long-tailed rodent
34. Australian explorer
36. Norwegian name of Norway
39. Frozen treats
41. American Indian
43. Not any
44. Belonging to them
46. Carried
48. Expire
49. Walk wearily
51. Prudes
53. Orators
56. America (Abbr)
57. Even (poet.)
58. Dismantle
64. Soft cheese
66. Back of neck
67. Eskimo dwelling
68. Looking skeletal
69. Skein of thread
70. Advances money
71. Verge
72. Seize
73. Stow away

DOWN
1. Juniper
2. River in central England
3. List of dishes
4. Speedy
5. Brooks
6. Festival
7. Single entity
8. Short dresses
9. Sailing vessels
10. Greek goddess of the dawn
11. Highway in Italy
12. Stenographer
13. Chemical compound
21. Indian peasants
22. Proper word
26. Lighting gas
27. Subpoena
28. Apiece
29. Becoming more precipitous
30. Matching outfit
31. Band
35. Ballet skirt
37. Smile
38. Sight organs
40. River sediment
42. African ground squirrel
45. Crucifix
47. Uses a still
50. Soak
52. Aim
53. Hebrew teacher
54. Biblical king
55. Fish covering
59. Candid
60. Salamander
61. Arm bone
62. Food fish
63. Nonsense
65. Organ of sight

Puzzle 120

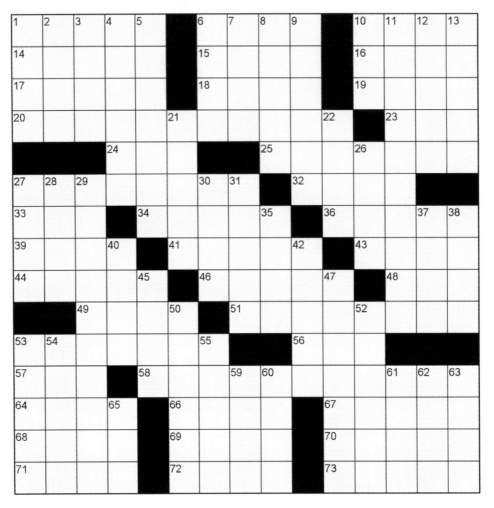

ACROSS
1. Sugary
6. A few
10. Woman who killed Sisera
14. Climbing vine
15. Raccoon
16. Sea eagle
17. Protective kitchen garment
18. Northern arm of the Black Sea
19. Periodic movement of the sea
20. Body of gendarmes
23. Arab market
24. Mature
25. Calms
27. Professional schools
32. Starch used in puddings
33. Atomic mass unit
34. Pertaining to a ramus
36. Birthplace of Muhammad
39. Having wealth
41. Citrus fruits
43. Dull
44. Eye sores
46. Hauled behind
48. Primate
49. Drop
51. Dependent on a drug
53. Green gem
56. North American nation
57. Spoil
58. Gelatin confection
64. Jelly-like mass
66. Sulk
67. Guy
68. Sewing case
69. Once again
70. Russian revolutionary leader
71. Coarse file
72. Stitched
73. Bordered

DOWN
1. Metal dross
2. Towel off
3. Merit
4. Without nodes
5. Scarlet bird
6. Swindle
7. Exude slowly
8. Anchors vessel
9. Is jealous of
10. Black
11. A noble
12. Invest
13. Welsh vegetables
21. Majestic
22. Dutch cheese
26. Old
27. Vehicles
28. Leave out
29. Providing light
30. Send forth
31. South Pacific Islands
35. Obscene
37. Cloak
38. In bed
40. Perceive sound
42. Herb
45. Shut with force
47. Incapacitate
50. South American beasts
52. Visited
53. Live coal
54. Mediterranean island
55. Honeybee
59. Vomit
60. Chopped
61. Lengthy
62. Migrant farm worker
63. Travel
65. Beep horn

Answer 1

Answer 2

Answer 3

Answer 4

Answer 5

Answer 6

Answer 7

Answer 8

Answer 9

Answer 10

Answer 11

Answer 12

Answer 13

Answer 14

Answer 15

Answer 16

Answer 17

Answer 18

Answer 19

Answer 20

Answer 21

Answer 22

Answer 23

Answer 24

Answer 25

Answer 26

Answer 27

Answer 28

Answer 29

Answer 30

Answer 31

Answer 32

Answer 33

Answer 34

Answer 35

Answer 36

Answer 37

Answer 38

Answer 39

Answer 40

Answer 41

Answer 42

Answer 43

Answer 44

Answer 45

Answer 46

Answer 47

Answer 48

Answer 49

Answer 50

Answer 51

Answer 52

Answer 53

Answer 54

Answer 55

Answer 56

Answer 57

Answer 58

Answer 59

Answer 60

Answer 61

Answer 62

Answer 63

Answer 64

Answer 65

Answer 66

Answer 67

Answer 68

Answer 69

Answer 70

Answer 71

Answer 72

Answer 73

S	O	R	T	■	L	A	V	A	■	S	L	O	S	H
I	L	I	A	■	E	B	O	N	■	V	O	L	T	E
R	I	N	K	■	S	A	L	T	C	E	L	L	A	R
E	D	G	E	W	I	S	E	■	A	L	L	A	Y	S
■	■	■	■	R	O	E	■	S	I	T	S	■	■	■
R	A	I	S	O	N	D	E	T	R	E	■	N	O	D
E	B	O	A	T	S	■	T	U	N	■	S	A	G	O
S	I	D	L	E	■	A	N	D	■	P	E	W	I	T
E	D	I	T	■	A	H	A	■	C	L	E	A	V	E
T	E	N	■	L	O	O	S	E	L	I	M	B	E	D
■	■	■	M	A	R	Y	■	D	E	E	■	■	■	■
E	F	F	O	R	T	■	J	I	M	D	A	N	D	Y
R	E	O	R	G	A	N	I	S	E	■	G	O	R	E
S	E	N	S	E	■	A	V	O	N	■	O	V	A	L
E	L	D	E	R	■	G	E	N	T	■	G	A	W	P

Answer 74

Answer 75

Answer 76

Answer 77

Answer 78

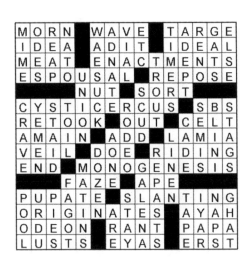

Answer 79

Answer 80

Answer 81

Answer 82

Answer 83

Answer 84

Answer 85

Answer 86

Answer 87

Answer 88

Answer 89

Answer 90

Answer 91

Answer 92

Answer 93

Answer 94

Answer 95

Answer 96

Answer 97

Answer 98

Answer 99

Answer 100

Answer 101

Answer 102

Answer 103

P	O	U	T	Y		C	H	A	P		S	C	U	M
E	G	R	E	T		O	A	T	H		K	A	L	E
A	L	E	R	T		I	N	T	O		I	N	C	A
R	E	A	R	R	A	N	G	I	N	G		N	E	T
			O	I	L		C	I	N	D	E	R	S	
A	L	T	R	U	I	S	M		C	A	U	L		
C	A	R		M	A	K	E	R		R	A	L	E	D
I	M	A	M		S	I	L	A	T		D	O	M	E
D	A	M	O	N		T	E	P	E	E		N	I	N
		P	O	U	F		E	T	E	R	N	I	T	Y
O	D	O	N	T	I	C		M	A	E				
S	O	L		S	E	L	F	A	S	S	U	R	E	D
C	L	I	P		R	E	A	D		U	R	E	D	O
A	C	N	E		C	A	R	D		R	A	N	G	E
R	E	E	D		E	R	O	S		E	L	D	E	R

Answer 104

Answer 105

Answer 106

Answer 107

Answer 108

Answer 109

Answer 110

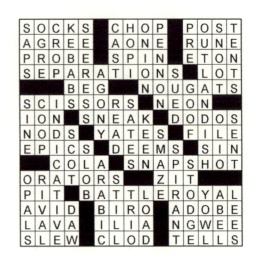

Answer 111

Answer 112

Answer 113

Answer 114

Answer 115

P	L	A	N	E	■	S	L	U	R	■	A	J	A	R
R	I	Y	A	L	■	H	O	N	E	■	S	O	S	O
O	L	I	V	E	■	I	R	I	S	■	K	U	D	U
D	Y	N	A	M	O	M	E	T	E	R	■	R	I	G
■	■	■	H	E	R	■	E	N	O	U	N	C	E	■
L	I	L	O	N	G	W	E	■	T	U	N	A	■	■
O	D	E	■	T	A	R	D	Y	■	T	I	L	T	S
F	L	O	W	■	N	A	G	O	R	■	T	I	R	E
T	Y	P	A	L	■	P	E	R	I	L	■	S	U	N
■	■	A	F	A	R	■	D	E	F	E	A	T	E	D
P	A	R	T	I	E	S	■	■	L	O	P	■	■	■
A	I	D	■	C	A	N	D	L	E	P	O	W	E	R
P	O	E	T	■	S	A	R	I	■	A	G	A	M	A
A	L	S	O	■	O	R	E	S	■	R	E	R	I	G
L	I	S	P	■	N	E	W	T	■	D	E	N	T	S

Answer 116

Answer 117

Answer 118

Answer 119

Answer 120

Imprint
Tim Rosenbladt
Carissa, Block 14, Flat 7A
Triq F. Vidal, Ibrag
SWQ 2471, Malta

Puzzles are created using Crossword Express

Made in the USA
Middletown, DE
26 October 2024